New Bilingual Visual Dictionary

English–Spanish

Milet

Milet Publishing
Smallfields Cottage, Cox Green
Rudgwick, Horsham, West Sussex
RH12 3DE England
info@milet.com
www.milet.com
www.milet.co.uk

First English–Spanish edition published by Milet Publishing in 2017

Copyright © Milet Publishing, 2017

ISBN 978 1 78508 893 3

Text by Sedat Turhan & Patricia Billings
Illustrated by Anna Martinez
Designed by Christangelos Seferiadis

Printed and bound in China by 1010 Printing International Ltd, March 2017.

falcon
halcón

eagle
águila

flamingo
flamingo

heron
garza

swan
cisne

pelican
pelícano

gull
gaviota

4

swallow
golondrina

lovebird
periquito

crow
cuervo

pigeon
pichón

robin
petirrojo

stork
cigüeña

ostrich
avestruz

peacock
pavo real

sparrow
gorrión

parrot
loro

wing
ala

beak
pico

owl
búho

claw
garra

woodpecker
pájaro carpintero

nest
nido

tail
cola

birdcage
jaula

vulture
buitre

egg
huevo

feather
pluma

pet
mascota

dog
perro

puppy
cachorro

pet bed
cama para mascota

cat
gato

kitten
gatito

collar
collar

crest
cresta

chick
pollito

hen
gallina

rooster
gallo

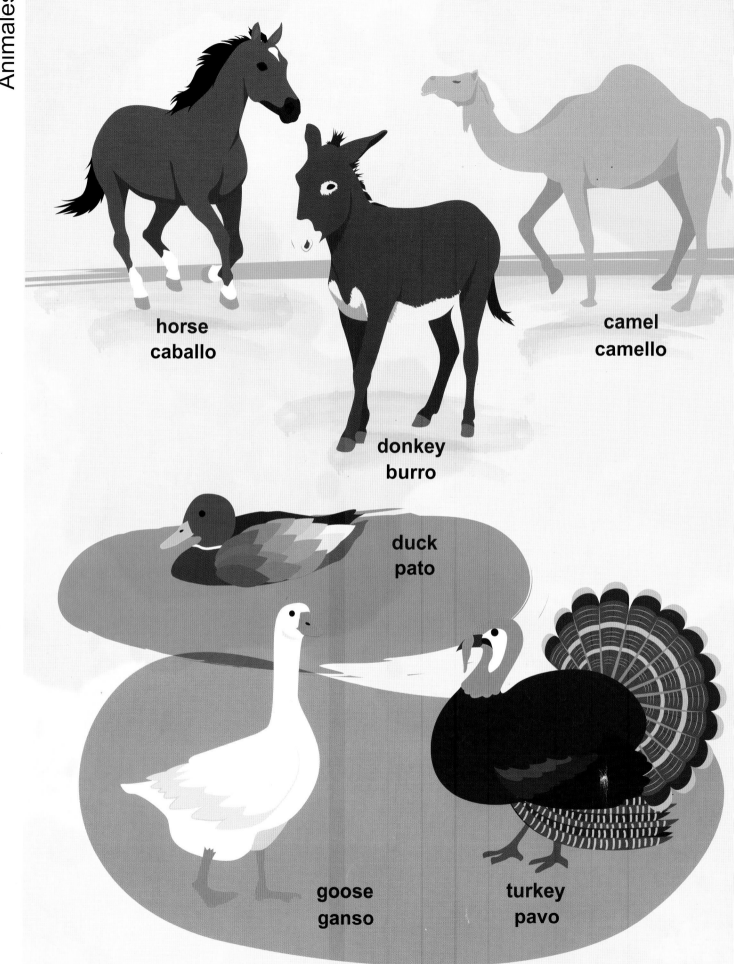

horse
caballo

donkey
burro

camel
camello

duck
pato

goose
ganso

turkey
pavo

barn
establo

cow
vaca

bull
toro

calf
becerro

pig
cerdo

sheep
oveja

lamb
cordero

goat
cabra

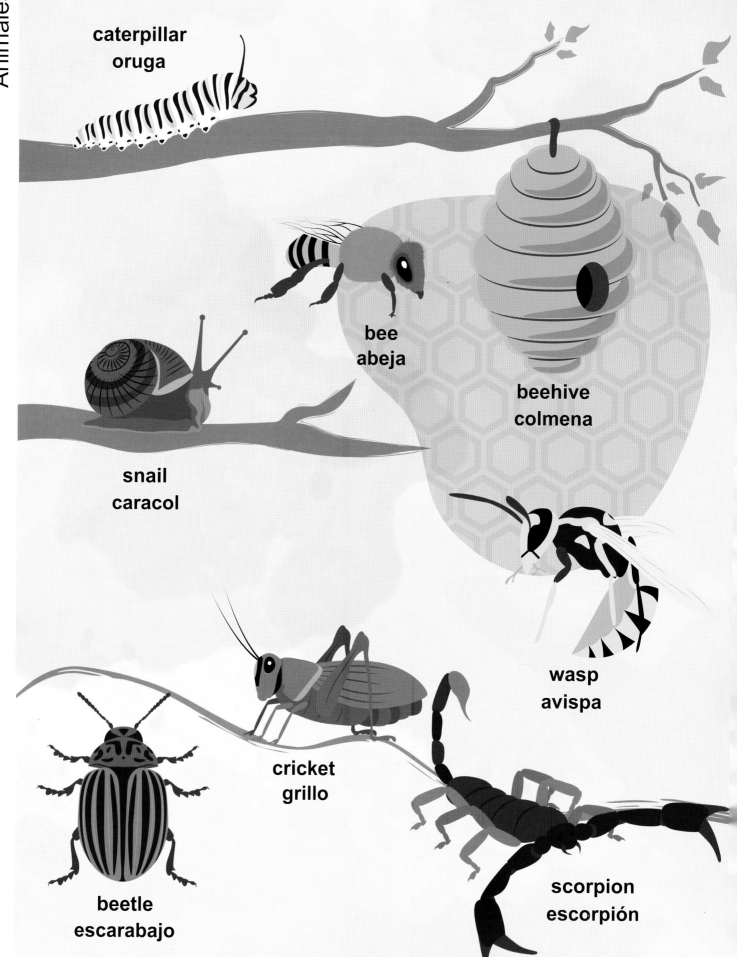

caterpillar
oruga

bee
abeja

beehive
colmena

snail
caracol

wasp
avispa

cricket
grillo

beetle
escarabajo

scorpion
escorpión

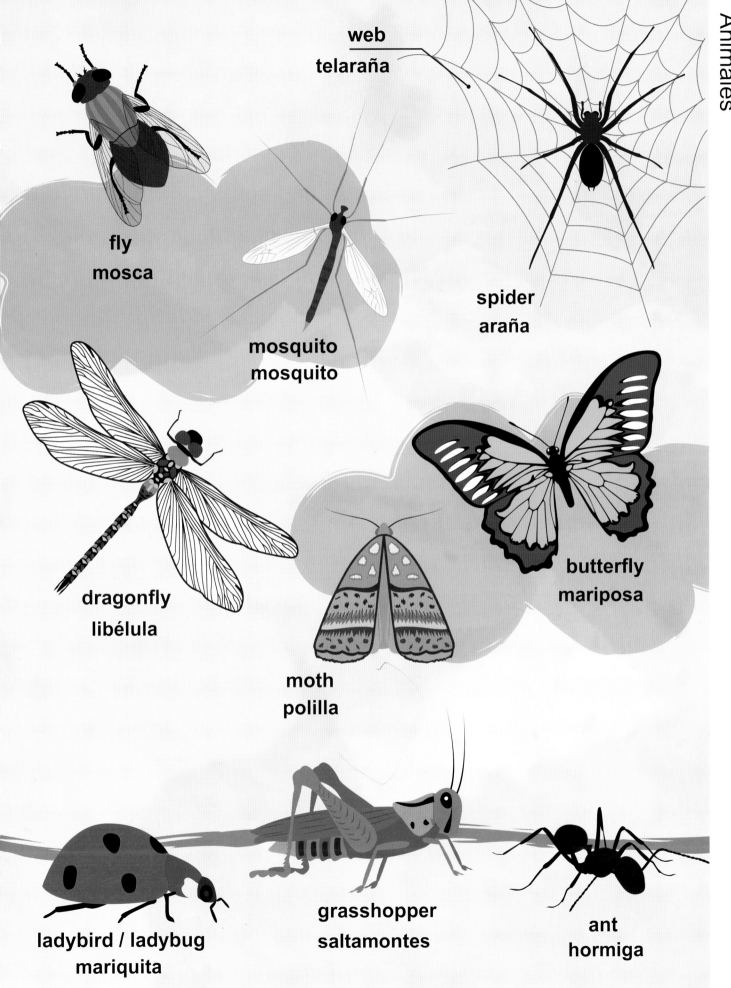

fly
mosca

web
telaraña

spider
araña

mosquito
mosquito

dragonfly
libélula

moth
polilla

butterfly
mariposa

ladybird / ladybug
mariquita

grasshopper
saltamontes

ant
hormiga

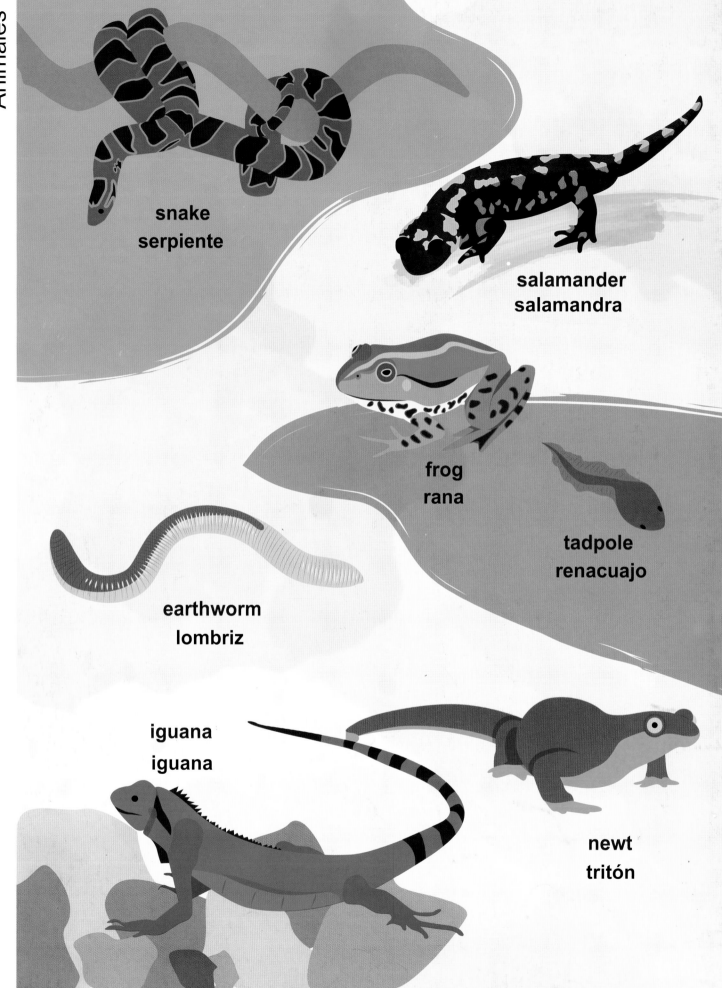

snake
serpiente

salamander
salamandra

frog
rana

tadpole
renacuajo

earthworm
lombriz

iguana
iguana

newt
tritón

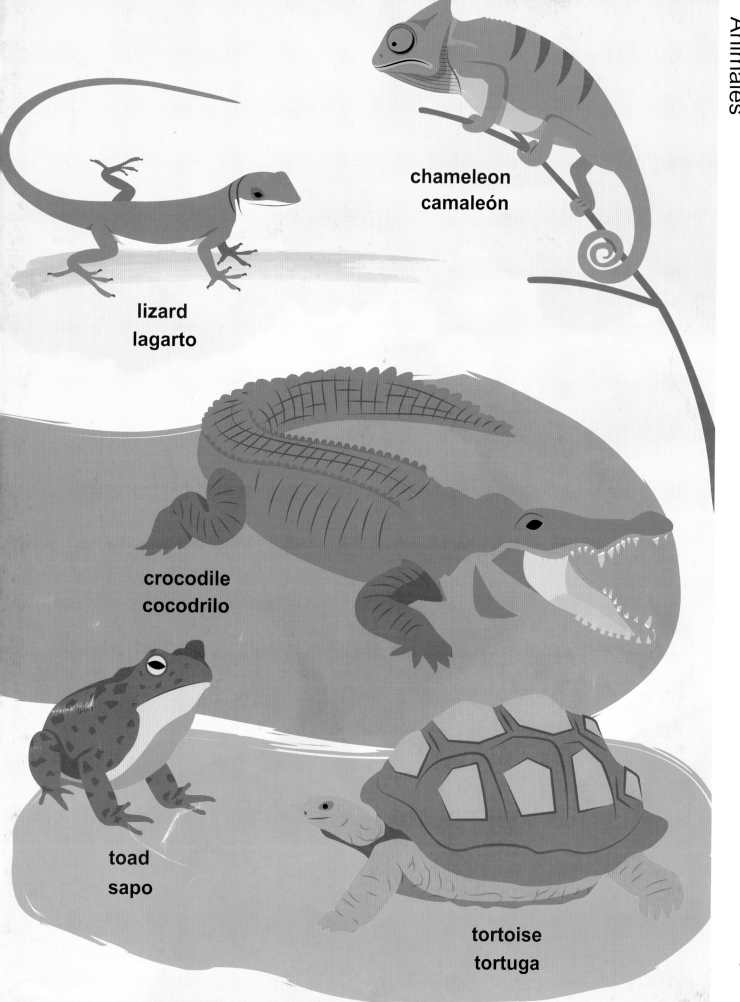

chameleon
camaleón

lizard
lagarto

crocodile
cocodrilo

toad
sapo

tortoise
tortuga

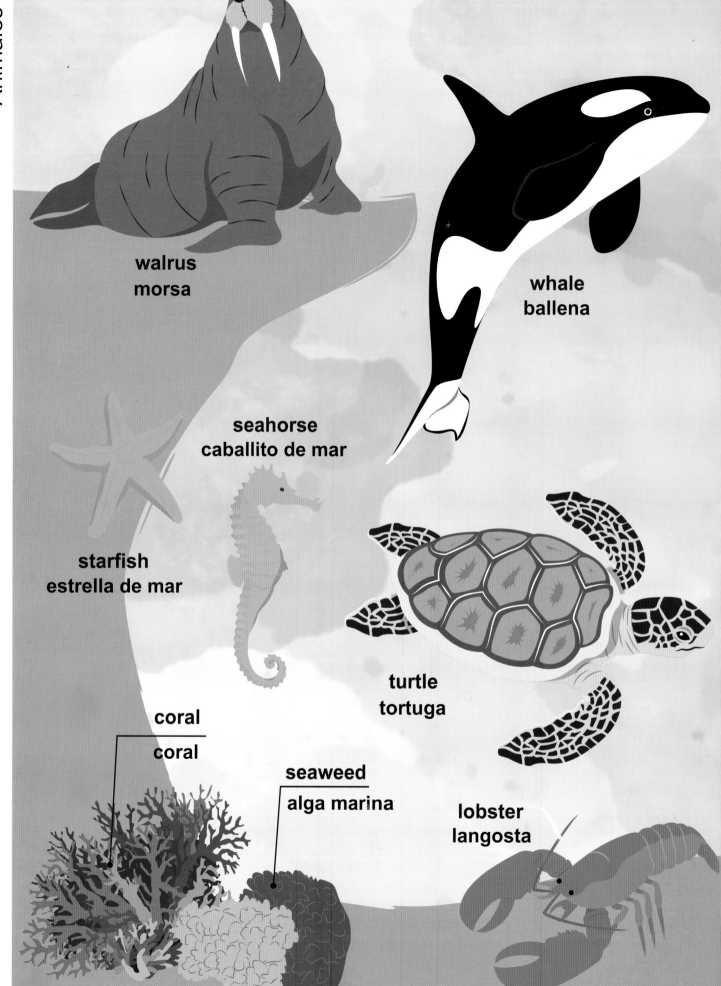

walrus
morsa

whale
ballena

seahorse
caballito de mar

starfish
estrella de mar

coral
coral

seaweed
alga marina

turtle
tortuga

lobster
langosta

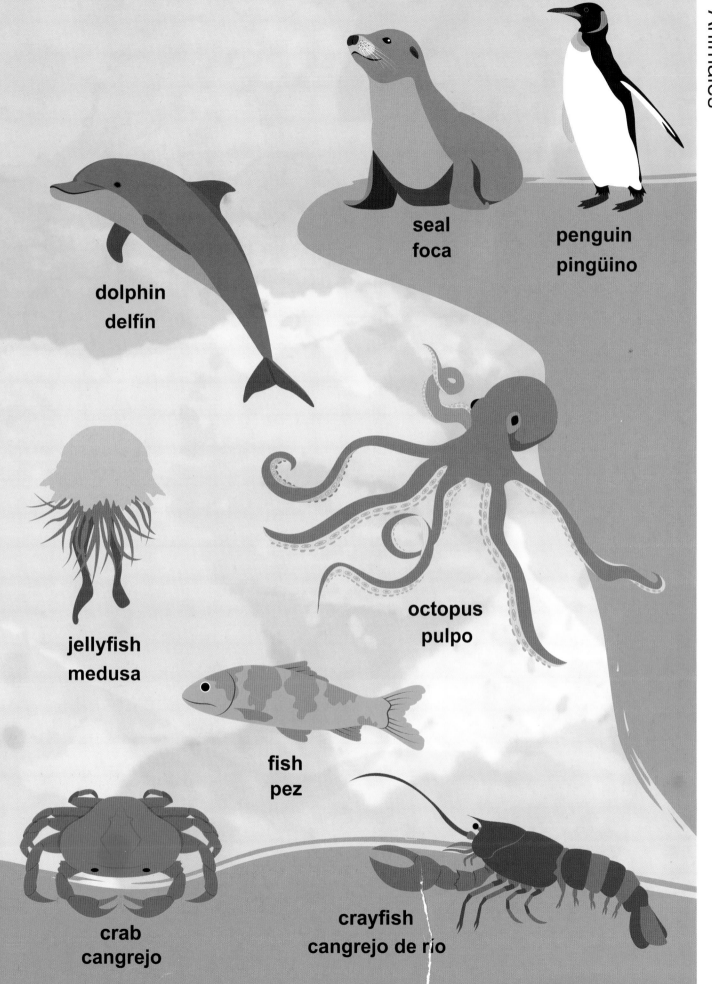

seal
foca

penguin
pingüino

dolphin
delfín

jellyfish
medusa

octopus
pulpo

fish
pez

crab
cangrejo

crayfish
cangrejo de río

koala
koala

bat
murciélago

kangaroo
canguro

raccoon
mapache

skunk
mofeta/zorrillo

llama
llama

bear
oso

polar bear
oso polar

elephant
elefante

tusk
colmillo

trunk
trompa

panda
panda

fox
zorro

wolf
lobo

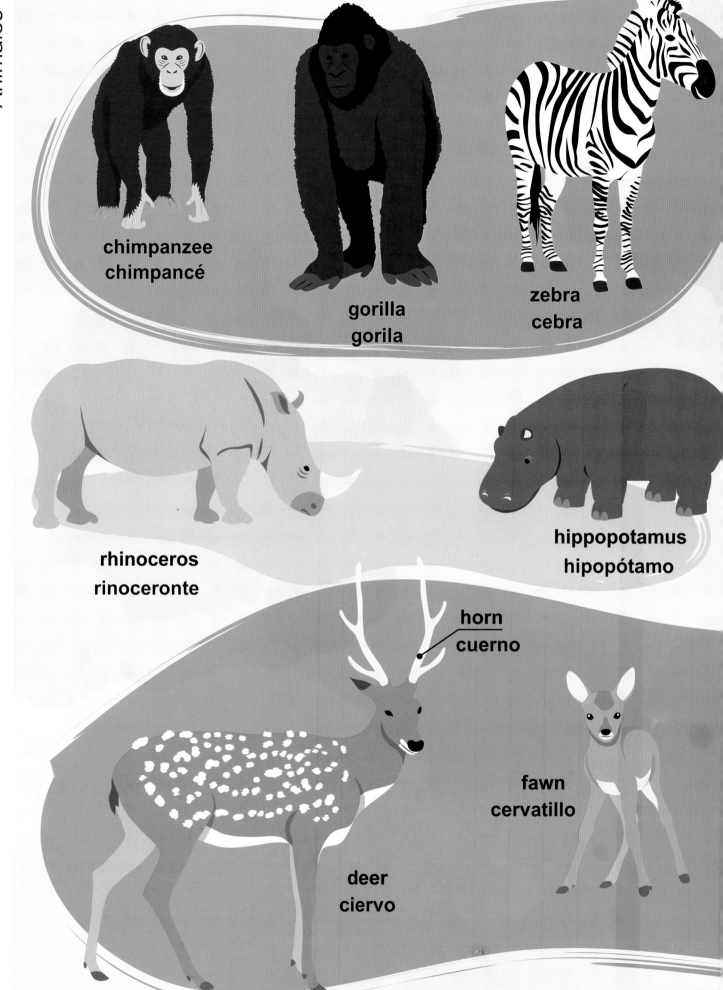

chimpanzee
chimpancé

gorilla
gorila

zebra
cebra

rhinoceros
rinoceronte

hippopotamus
hipopótamo

horn
cuerno

fawn
cervatillo

deer
ciervo

giraffe
jirafa

leopard
leopardo

tiger
tigre

mane
melena

lion
león

cub
cachorro

mole
topo

hedgehog
erizo

mouse
ratón

tail
cola

rat
rata

squirrel
ardilla

rabbit
conejo

otter
nutria

body
cuerpo

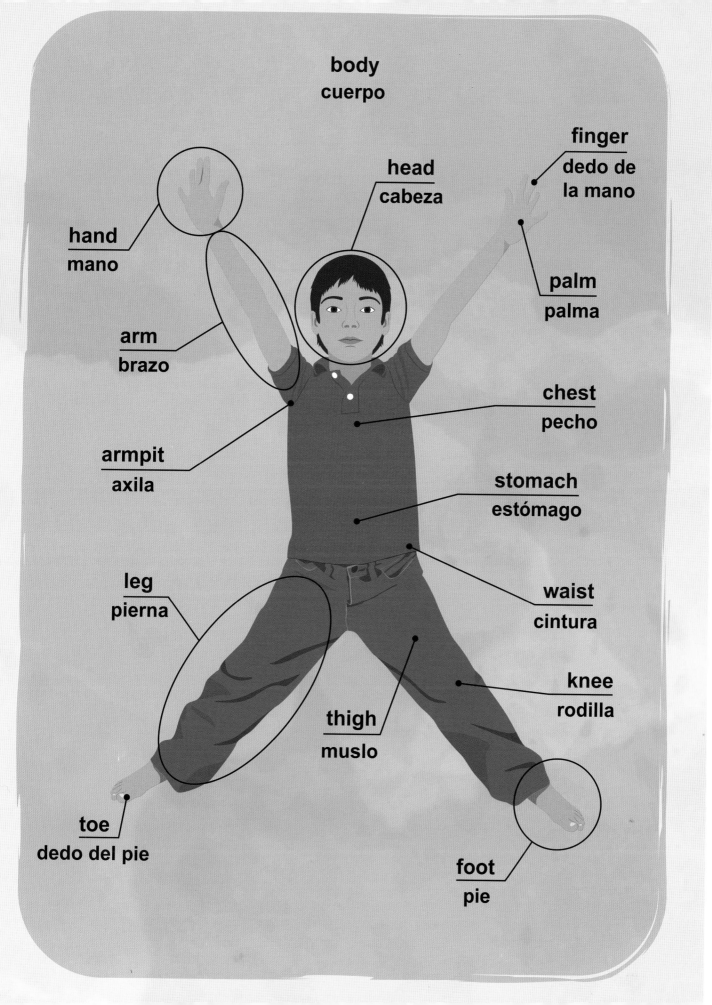

head
cabeza

finger
**dedo de
la mano**

hand
mano

palm
palma

arm
brazo

chest
pecho

armpit
axila

stomach
estómago

leg
pierna

waist
cintura

knee
rodilla

thigh
muslo

toe
dedo del pie

foot
pie

face
cara

eyebrow
ceja

hair
pelo

forehead
frente

eyelid
párpado

eye
ojo

eyelashes
pestañas

ear
oreja

cheek
mejilla

nose
nariz

lip
labio

mouth
boca

chin
barbilla

neck
cuello

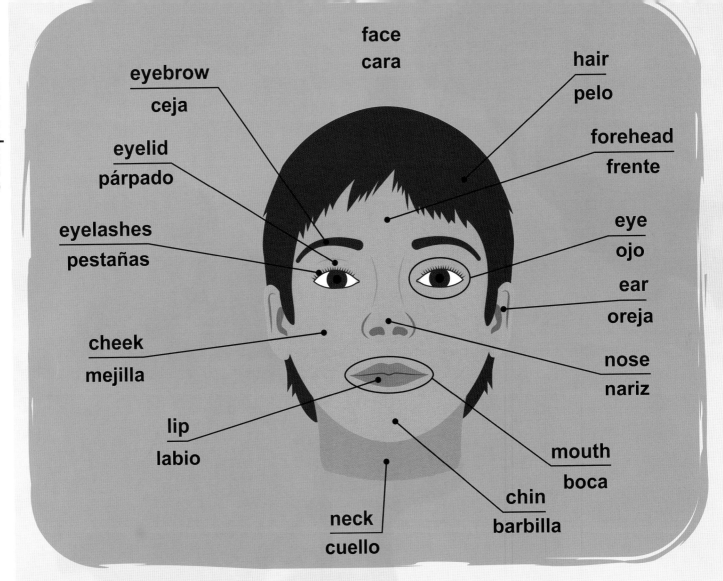

hand
mano

middle finger
dedo del medio

fingernail
uña

ring finger
dedo anular

index finger
dedo índice

little finger
dedo meñique

thumb
pulgar

wrist
muñeca

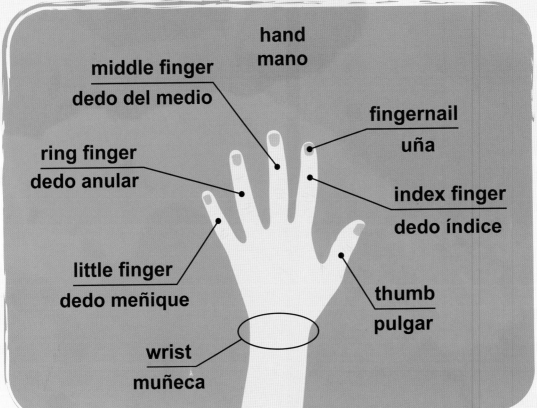

fingerprint
huella dactilar

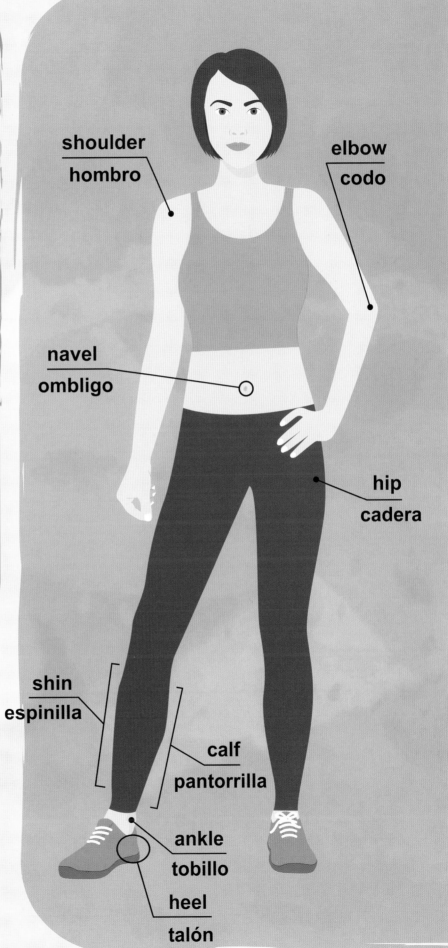

skeleton
esqueleto

skull
cráneo

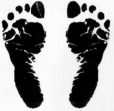

footprints
huellas

shoulder
hombro

elbow
codo

navel
ombligo

hip
cadera

shin
espinilla

calf
pantorrilla

ankle
tobillo

heel
talón

apartment building
condominio /
edificio de apartamentos

roof
techo

window
ventana

house
casa

wall
pared

chimney
chimenea

attic
ático

door
puerta

ground floor
planta baja

steps
escalones

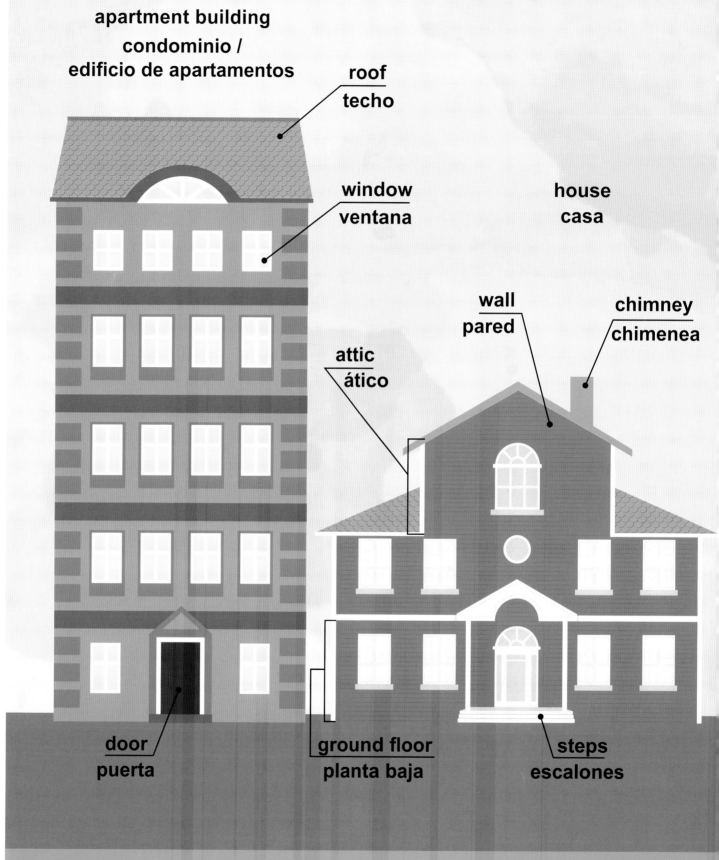

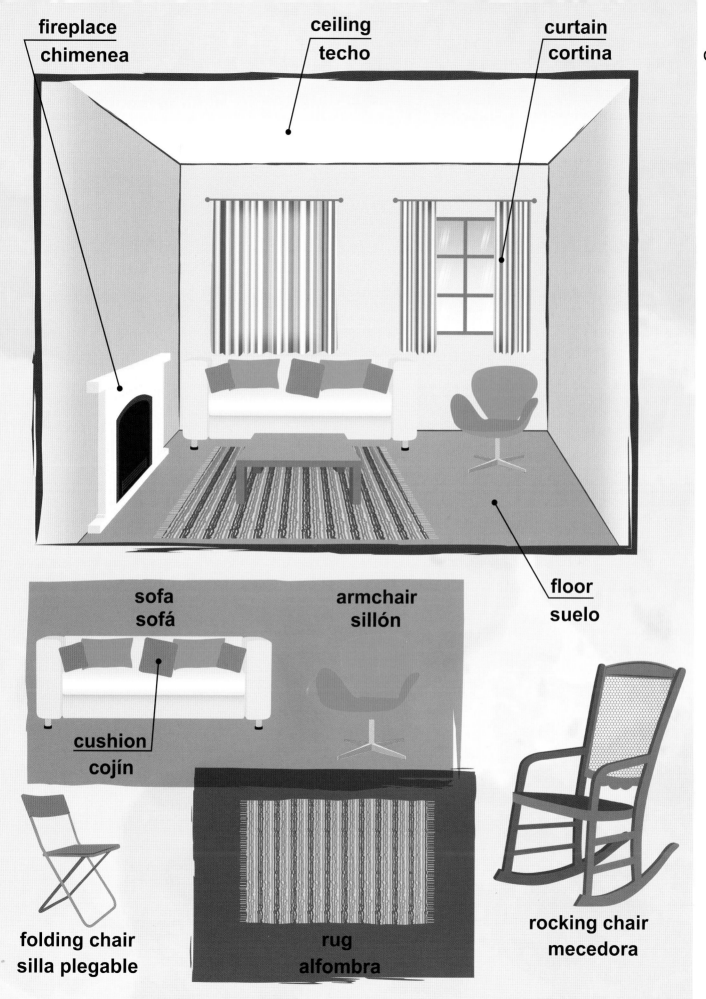

fireplace
chimenea

ceiling
techo

curtain
cortina

floor
suelo

sofa
sofá

armchair
sillón

cushion
cojín

folding chair
silla plegable

rug
alfombra

rocking chair
mecedora

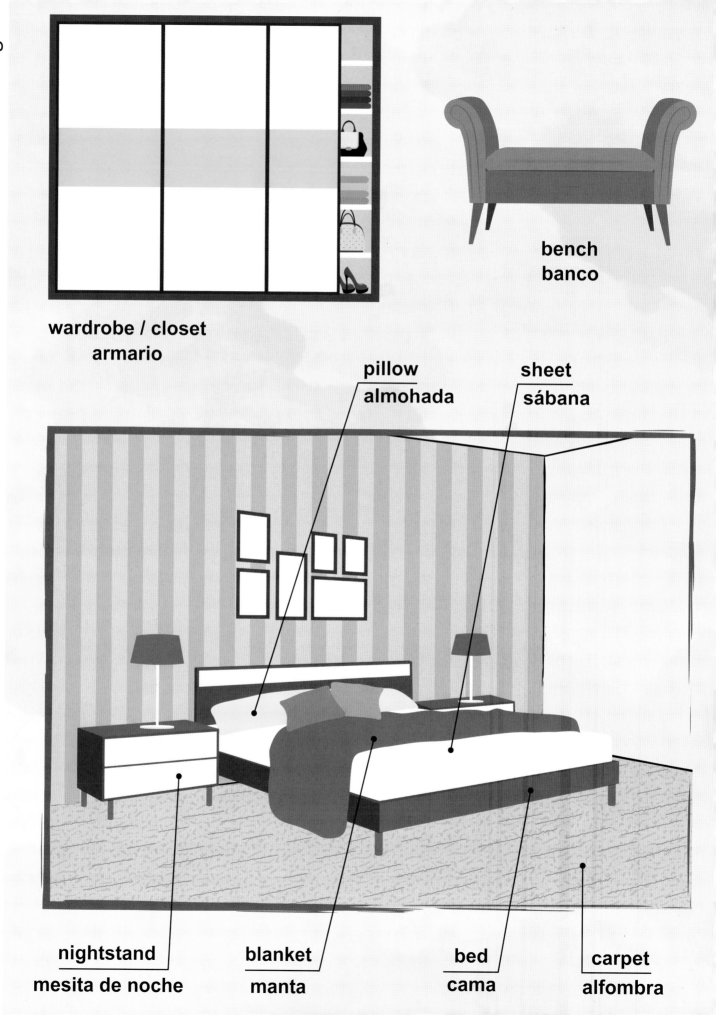

wardrobe / closet
armario

bench
banco

pillow
almohada

sheet
sábana

nightstand
mesita de noche

blanket
manta

bed
cama

carpet
alfombra

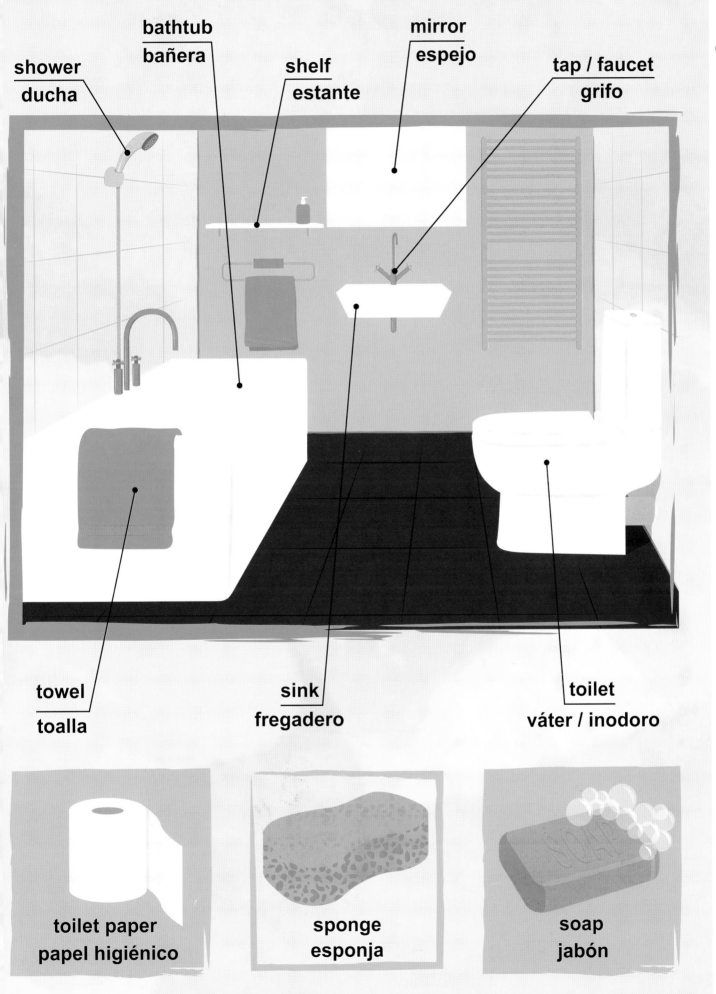

shower
ducha

bathtub
bañera

shelf
estante

mirror
espejo

tap / faucet
grifo

towel
toalla

sink
fregadero

toilet
váter / inodoro

toilet paper
papel higiénico

sponge
esponja

soap
jabón

console
consola

chair
silla

ceiling lamp
lámpara de techo

dining table
mesa de comedor

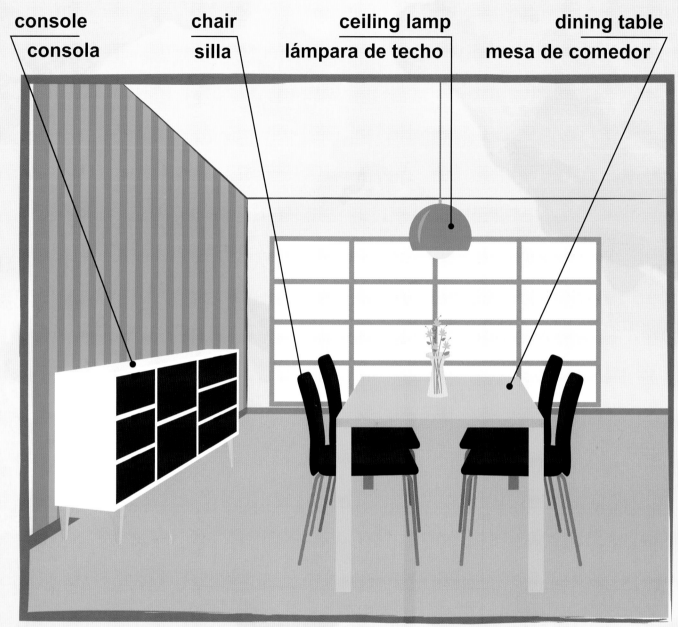

cabinet
armario

place setting
servicio de mesa

stool
taburete

range hood
campana extractora

oven
horno

drawer
cajón

cabinet
alacena

refrigerator
nevera

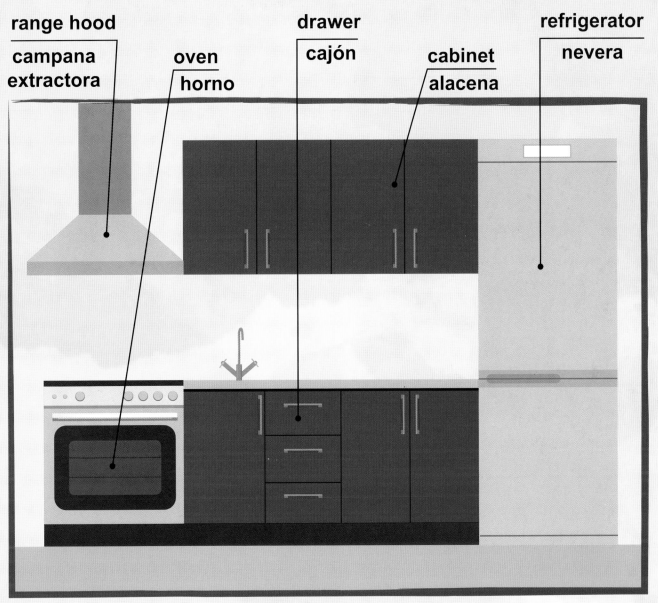

frying pan
sartén

bowl
tazón

pot
olla

slow cooker
olla de cocción lenta

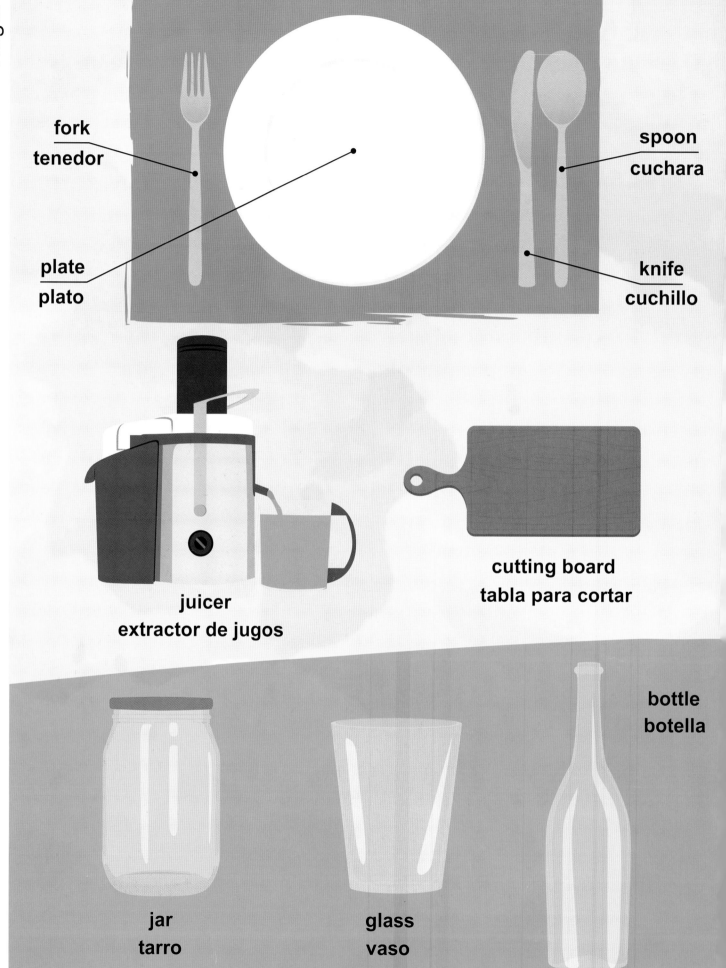

fork
tenedor

spoon
cuchara

plate
plato

knife
cuchillo

juicer
extractor de jugos

cutting board
tabla para cortar

bottle
botella

jar
tarro

glass
vaso

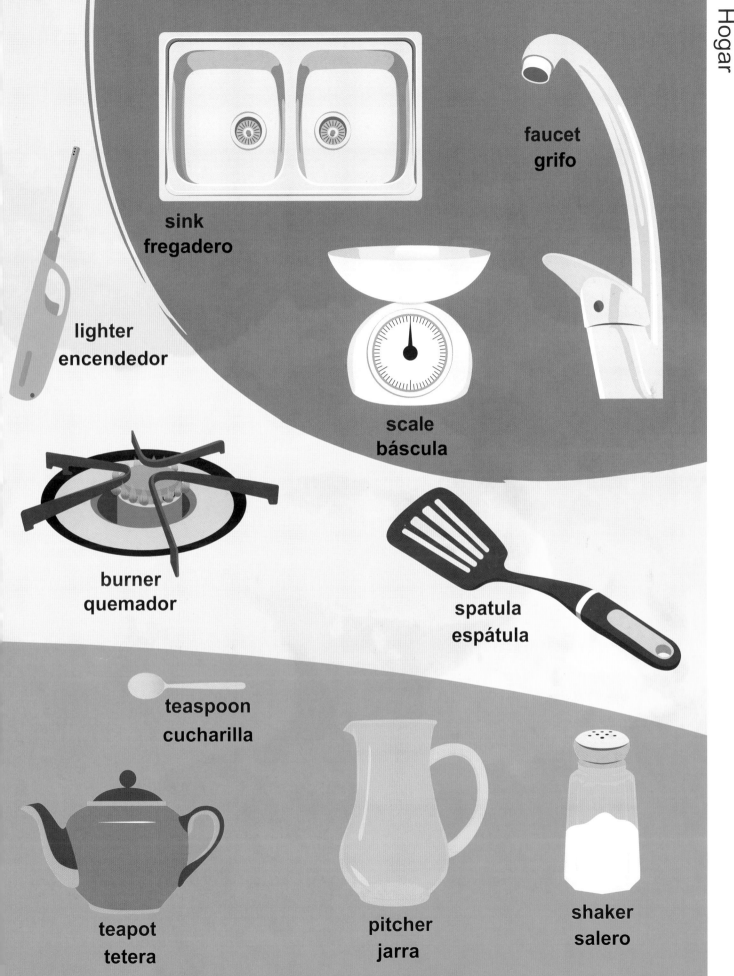

sink
fregadero

faucet
grifo

lighter
encendedor

scale
báscula

burner
quemador

spatula
espátula

teaspoon
cucharilla

teapot
tetera

pitcher
jarra

shaker
salero

mixer
batidora

toaster oven
horno tostador

food processor
procesador de
alimentos

blender
licuadora

toaster
tostador

microwave oven
horno microondas

dishwasher
lavavajillas

washing machine
lavadora

duster
plumero

iron
plancha

vacuum cleaner
aspiradora

ceiling fan
ventilador de techo

chandelier
candelabro

spotlight
foco

table lamp
lámpara

floor lamp
lámpara de piso

desk lamp
lámpara de escritorio

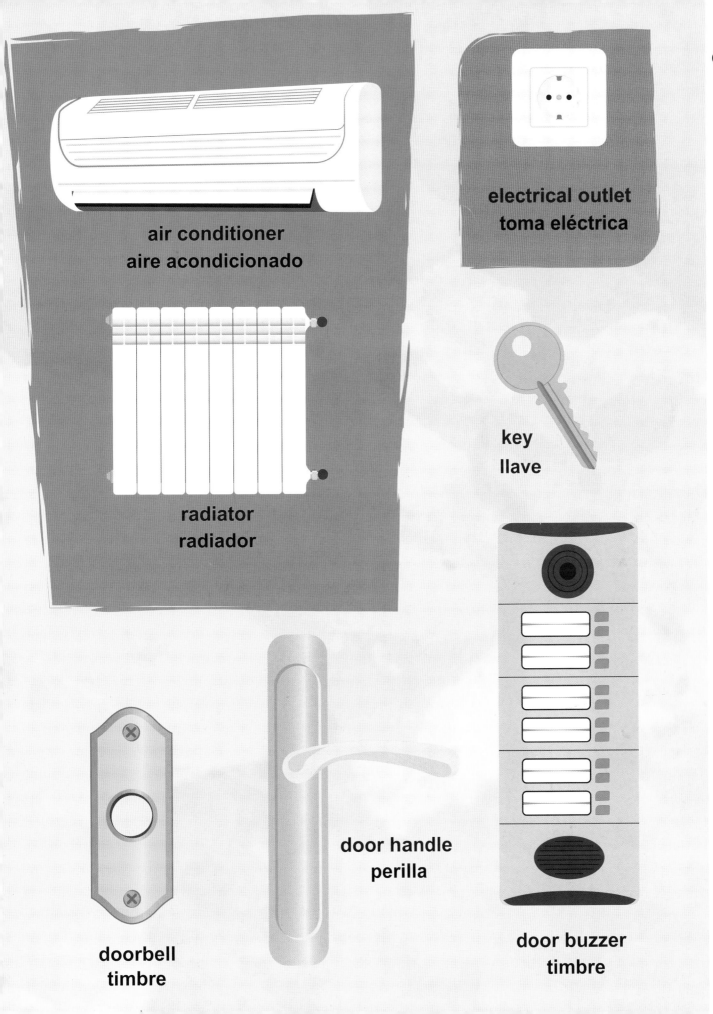

air conditioner
aire acondicionado

electrical outlet
toma eléctrica

radiator
radiador

key
llave

doorbell
timbre

door handle
perilla

door buzzer
timbre

35

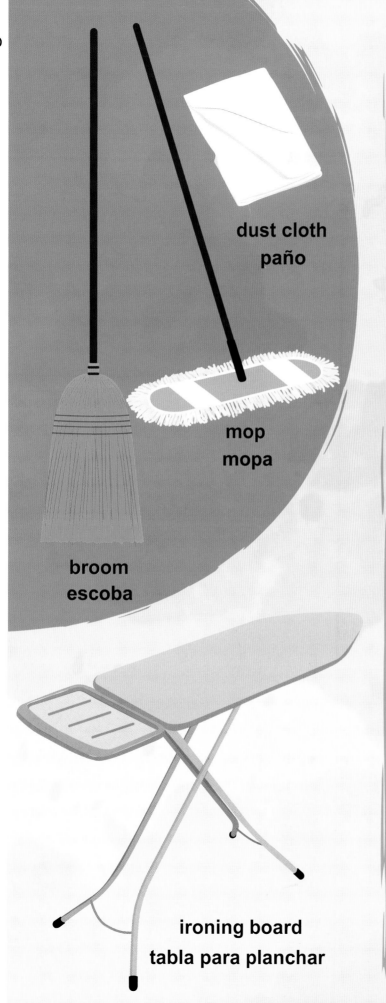

dust cloth
paño

mop
mopa

broom
escoba

ironing board
tabla para planchar

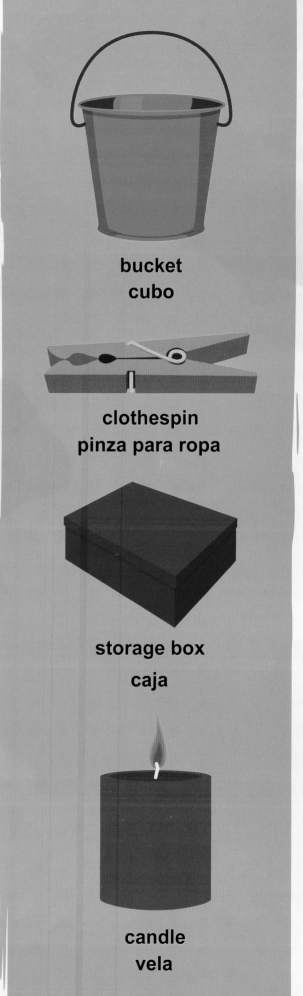

bucket
cubo

clothespin
pinza para ropa

storage box
caja

candle
vela

flowerpot
maceta

vase
florero

jerrycan
bidón

rubbish bag / garbage bag
bolsa para basura

doormat
alfombrilla

clock
reloj

basket
cesta

dress
vestido

blouse
blusa

skirt
falda

pumps
tacones

hat
sombrero

tie
corbata

bow tie
moño

suit
traje

shoes
zapatos

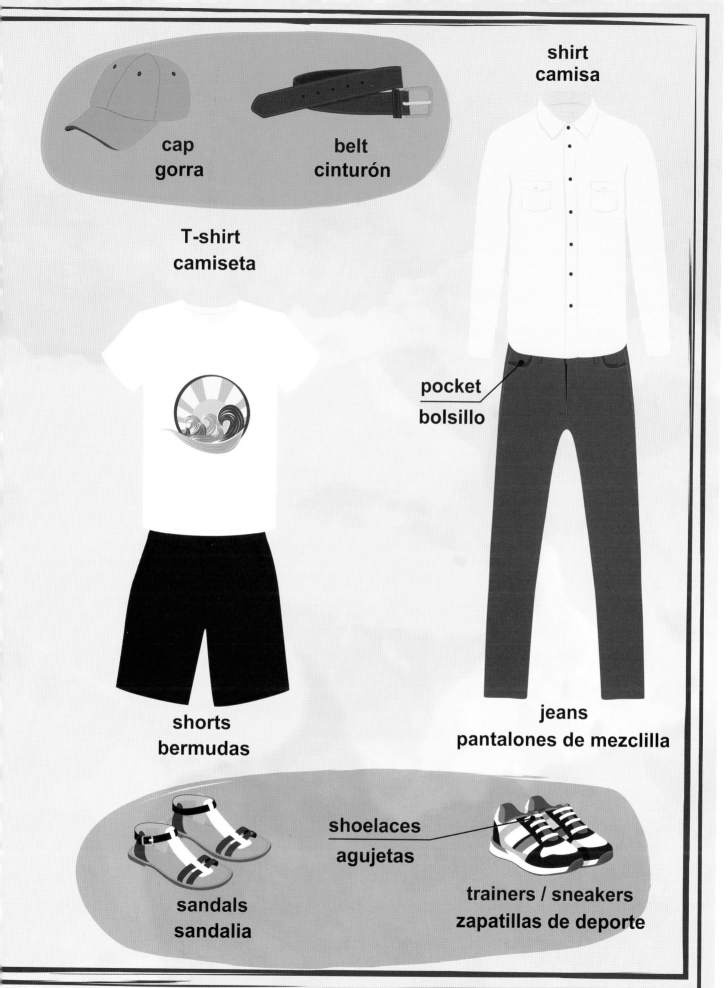

cap
gorra

belt
cinturón

shirt
camisa

T-shirt
camiseta

pocket
bolsillo

shorts
bermudas

jeans
pantalones de mezclilla

shoelaces
agujetas

sandals
sandalia

trainers / sneakers
zapatillas de deporte

swimsuit
traje de baño

flip-flops
chancletas

bathrobe
bata de baño

swim trunks
bermudas para nadar

slippers
pantuflas

sweater
sudadera

cardigan
rebeca

boots
botas

tracksuit
chándal

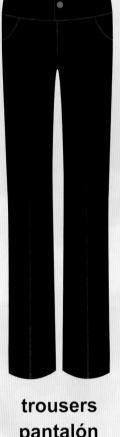

trousers
pantalón

coat
abrigo

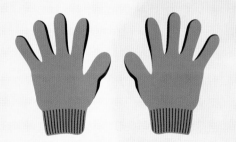

gloves
guantes

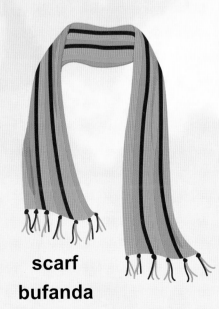

scarf
bufanda

socks
calcetines

clothes hanger
percha

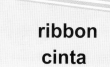

ribbon
cinta

pins
alfileres

button
botón

zipper
cremallera

thread
hilo

reel
carrete

sewing needle
aguja para coser

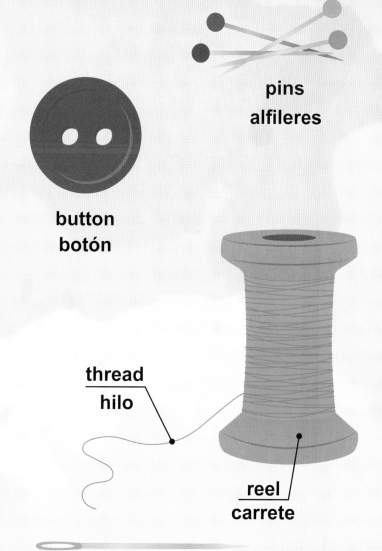

safety pin
pasador de seguridad

eyeglasses
gafas

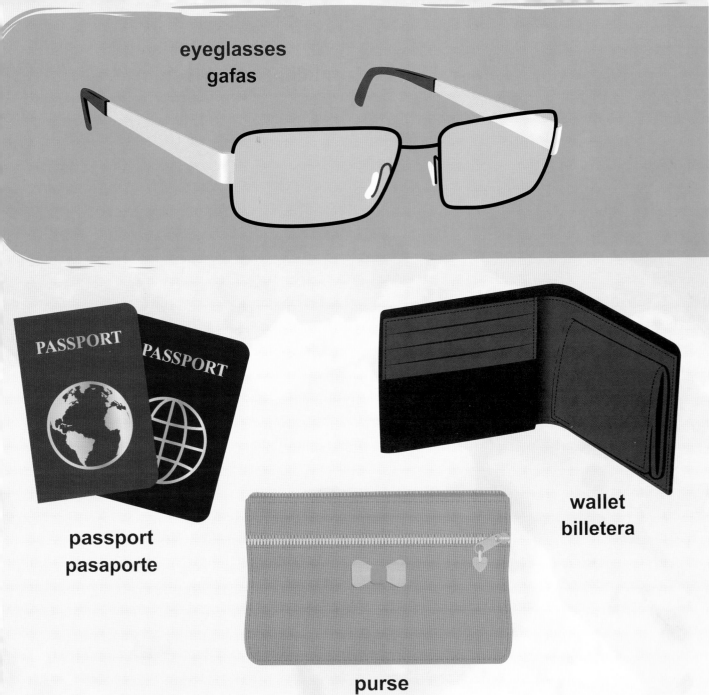

passport
pasaporte

wallet
billetera

purse
monedero

sunglasses
gafas de sol

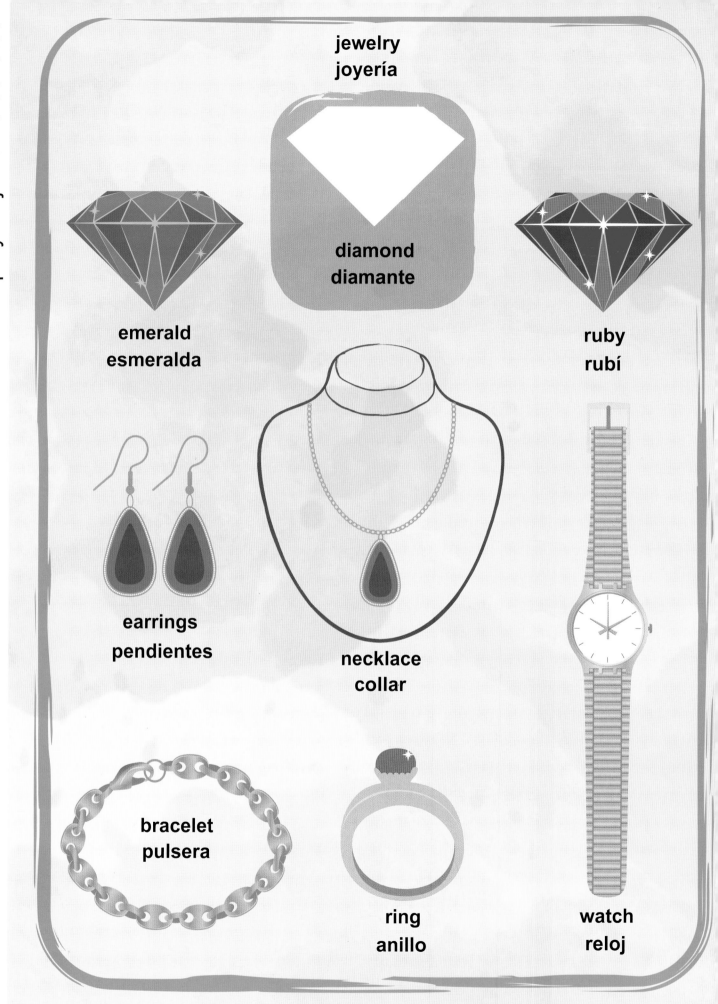

jewelry
joyería

diamond
diamante

emerald
esmeralda

ruby
rubí

earrings
pendientes

necklace
collar

bracelet
pulsera

ring
anillo

watch
reloj

umbrella
paraguas

briefcase
maletín

suitcase
maleta

handbag
bolso

backpack
mochila

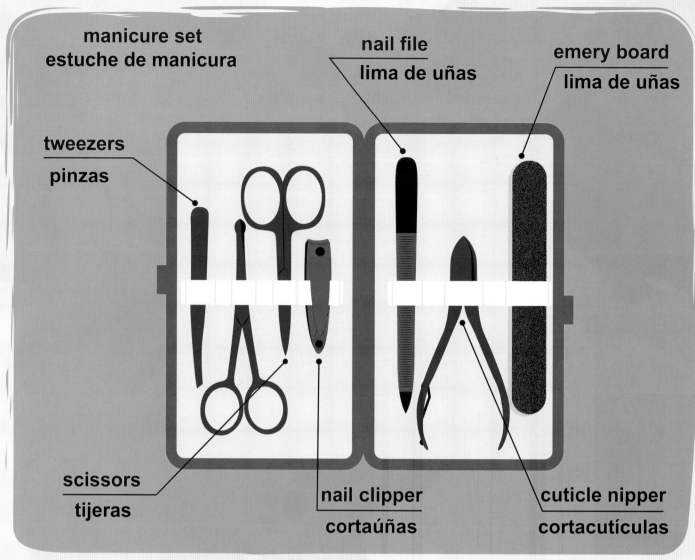

manicure set
estuche de manicura

nail file
lima de uñas

emery board
lima de uñas

tweezers
pinzas

scissors
tijeras

nail clipper
cortaúñas

cuticle nipper
cortacutículas

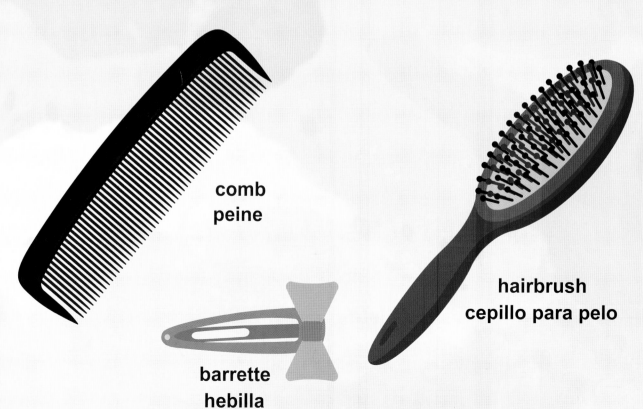

comb
peine

hairbrush
cepillo para pelo

barrette
hebilla

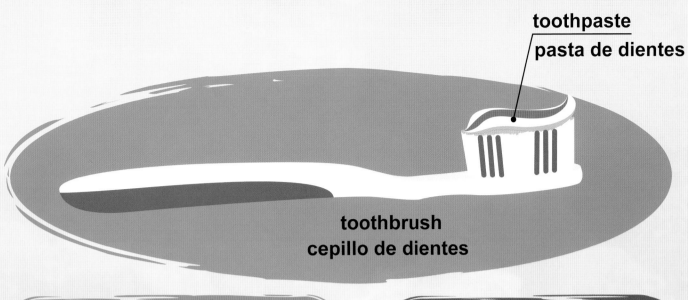

toothpaste
pasta de dientes

toothbrush
cepillo de dientes

perfume
perfume

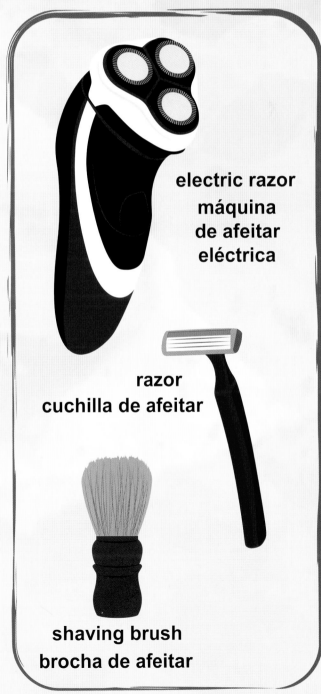

electric razor
máquina
de afeitar
eléctrica

razor
cuchilla de afeitar

shaving brush
brocha de afeitar

hair dryer
secador de pelo

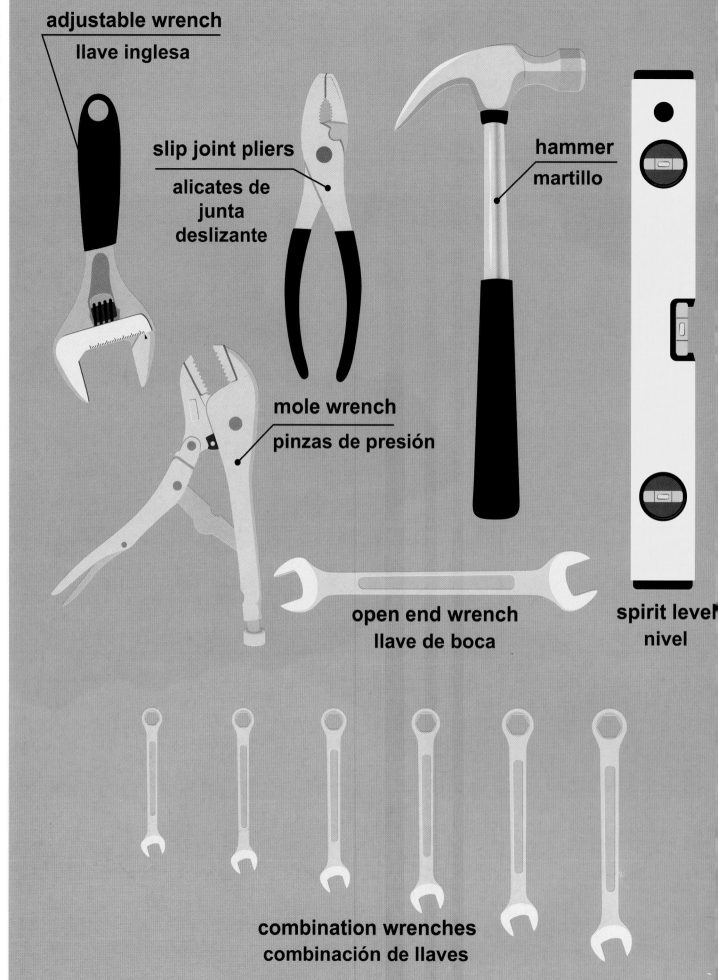

adjustable wrench
llave inglesa

slip joint pliers
alicates de
junta
deslizante

mole wrench
pinzas de presión

hammer
martillo

spirit level
nivel

open end wrench
llave de boca

combination wrenches
combinación de llaves

mallet
mazo

long nose pliers
**alicates de
punta larga**

screwdriver
destornillador

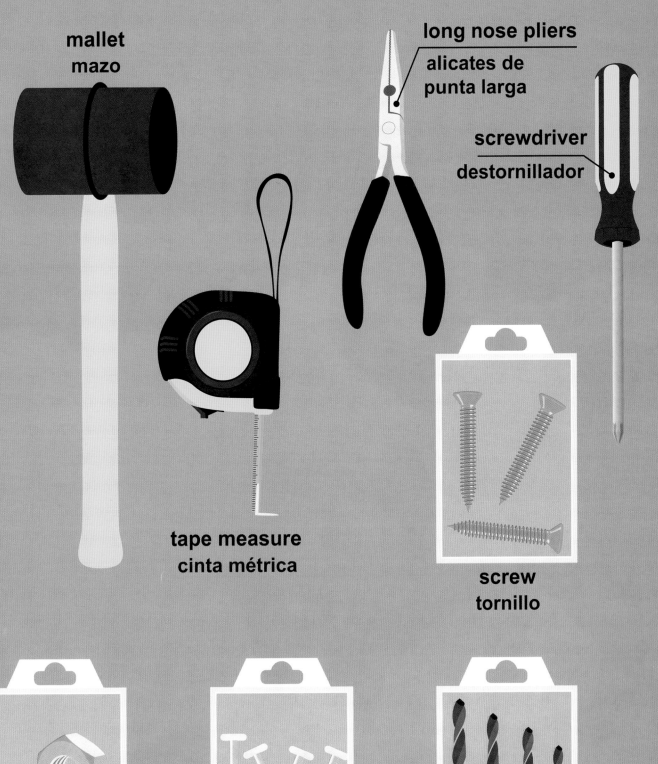

tape measure
cinta métrica

screw
tornillo

nut
tuerca

nail
clavo

drill bit
broca

chain
cadena

padlock
candado

battery
batería

plug
enchufe

toolbox
caja de herramientas

car battery
batería de coche

electric drill
taladro eléctrico

safety helmet
casco de seguridad

torch / flashlight
linterna

ladder
escalera

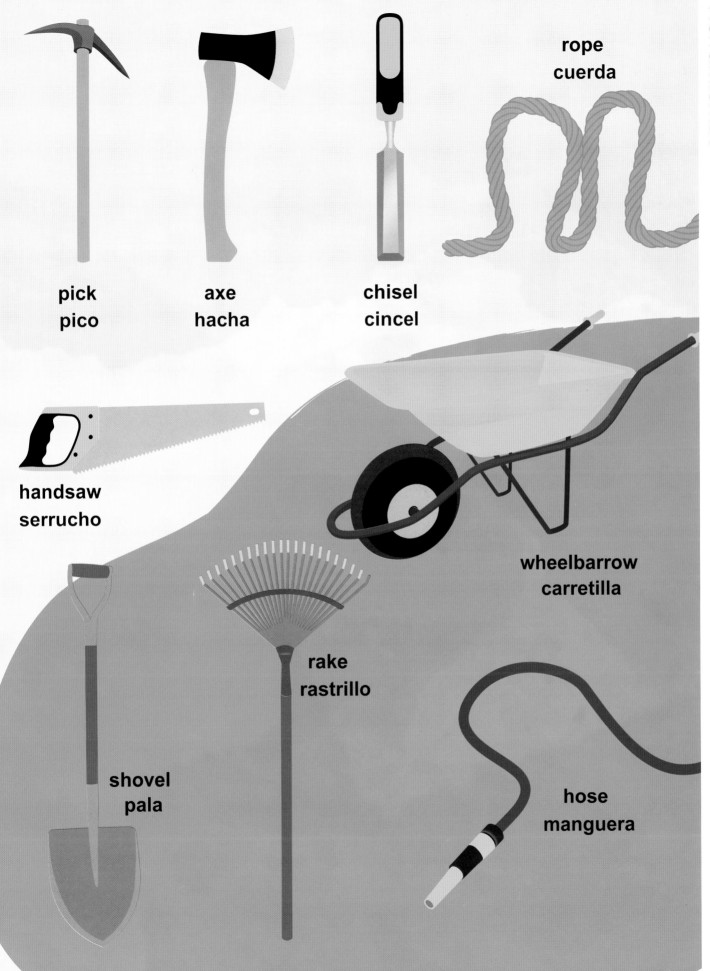

pick
pico

axe
hacha

chisel
cincel

rope
cuerda

handsaw
serrucho

wheelbarrow
carretilla

rake
rastrillo

shovel
pala

hose
manguera

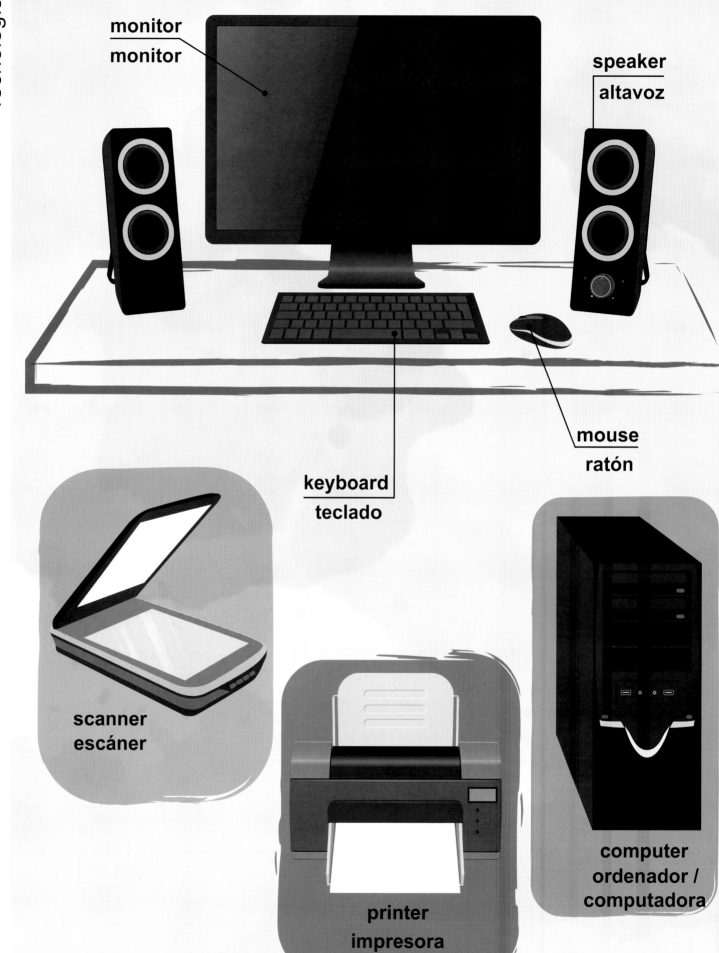

monitor
monitor

speaker
altavoz

mouse
ratón

keyboard
teclado

scanner
escáner

printer
impresora

computer
ordenador /
computadora

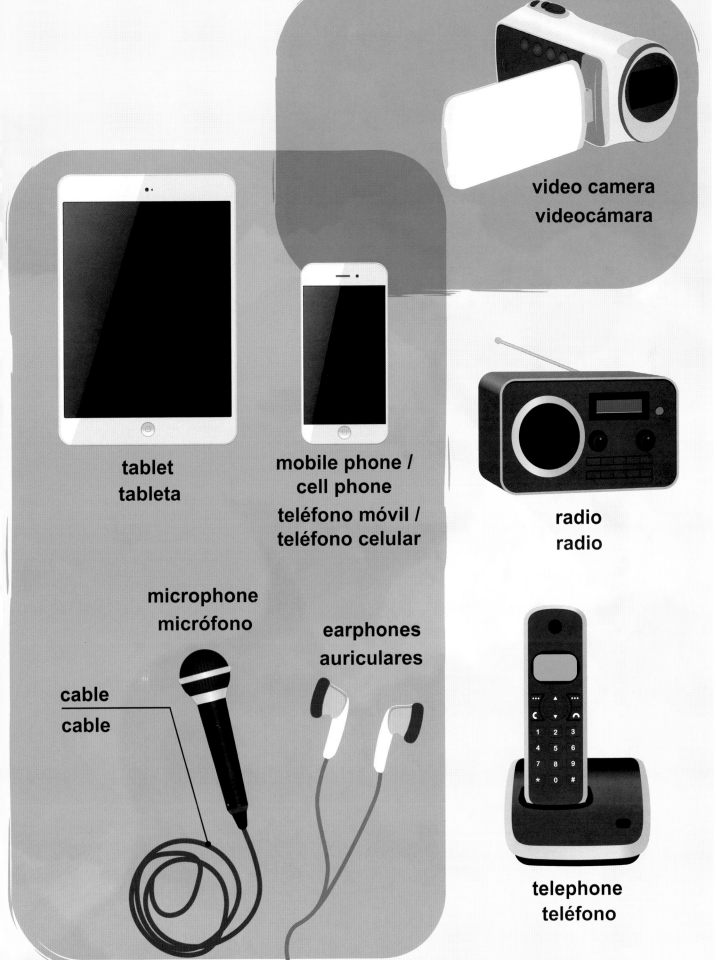

video camera
videocámara

tablet
tableta

mobile phone /
cell phone
teléfono móvil /
teléfono celular

radio
radio

microphone
micrófono

earphones
auriculares

cable
cable

telephone
teléfono

supermarket
supermercado

restaurant
restaurante

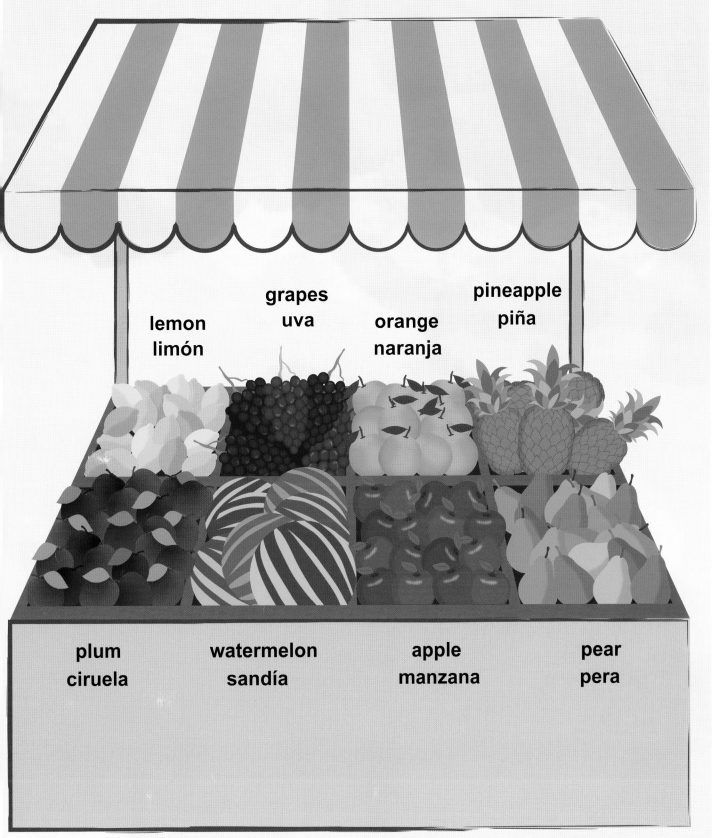

grapes
uva

lemon
limón

orange
naranja

pineapple
piña

plum
ciruela

watermelon
sandía

apple
manzana

pear
pera

apricot
albaricoque

peach
melocotón / durazno

banana
plátano

avocado
aguacate

cherry
cereza

strawberry
fresa

blackberry
mora

blueberry
arándano

raspberry
frambuesa

kiwi
kiwi

mandarin
mandarina

grapefruit
toronja

mango
mango

pomegranate
granada

quince
membrillo

melon
melón

coconut
coco

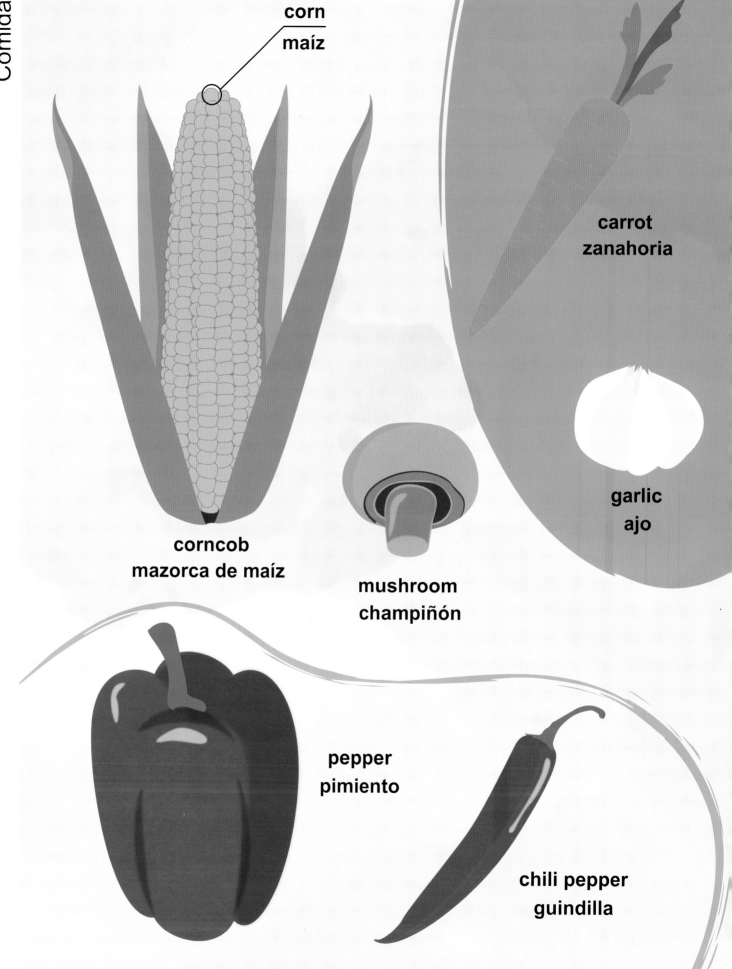

corn
maíz

corncob
mazorca de maíz

carrot
zanahoria

garlic
ajo

mushroom
champiñón

pepper
pimiento

chili pepper
guindilla

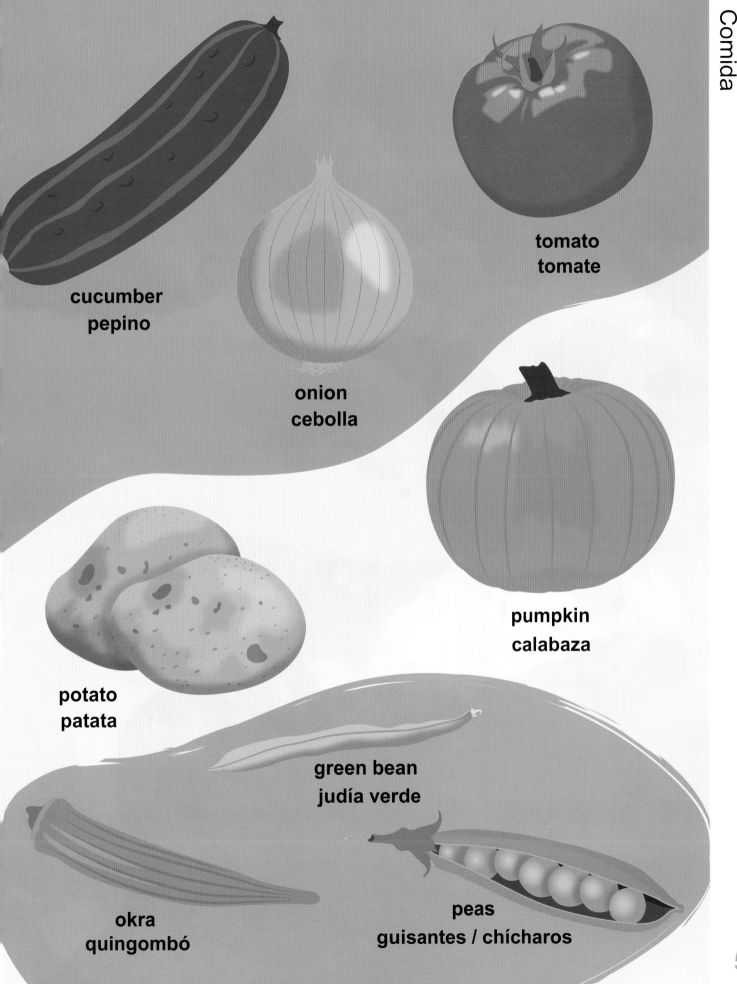

cucumber
pepino

onion
cebolla

tomato
tomate

pumpkin
calabaza

potato
patata

green bean
judía verde

okra
quingombó

peas
guisantes / chícharos

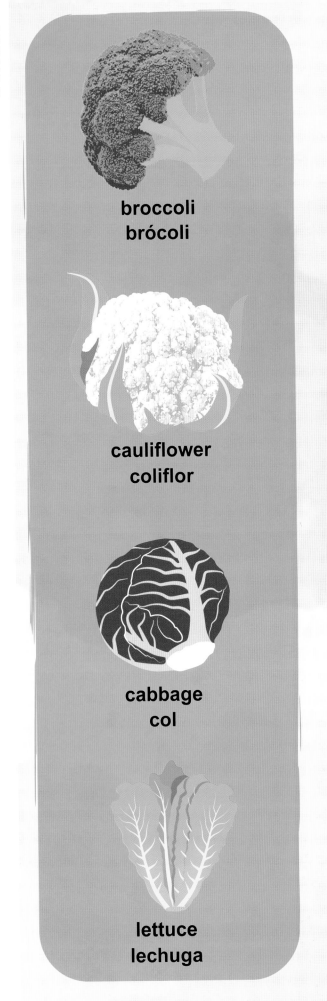

broccoli
brócoli

cauliflower
coliflor

cabbage
col

lettuce
lechuga

artichoke
alcachofa

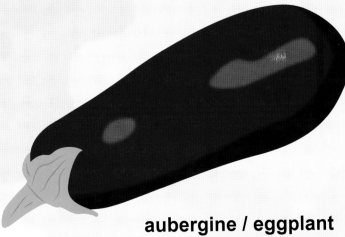

aubergine / eggplant
berenjena

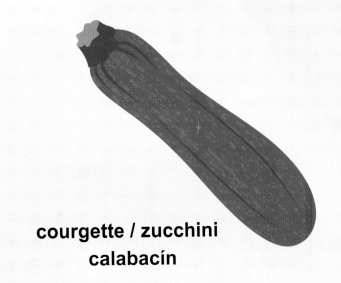

courgette / zucchini
calabacín

green onion
cebolleta /
cebollín

leek
puerro

celery
apio

spinach
espinaca

turnip
nabo

asparagus
espárrago

radish
rábano

dill
eneldo

mint
menta

parsley
perejil

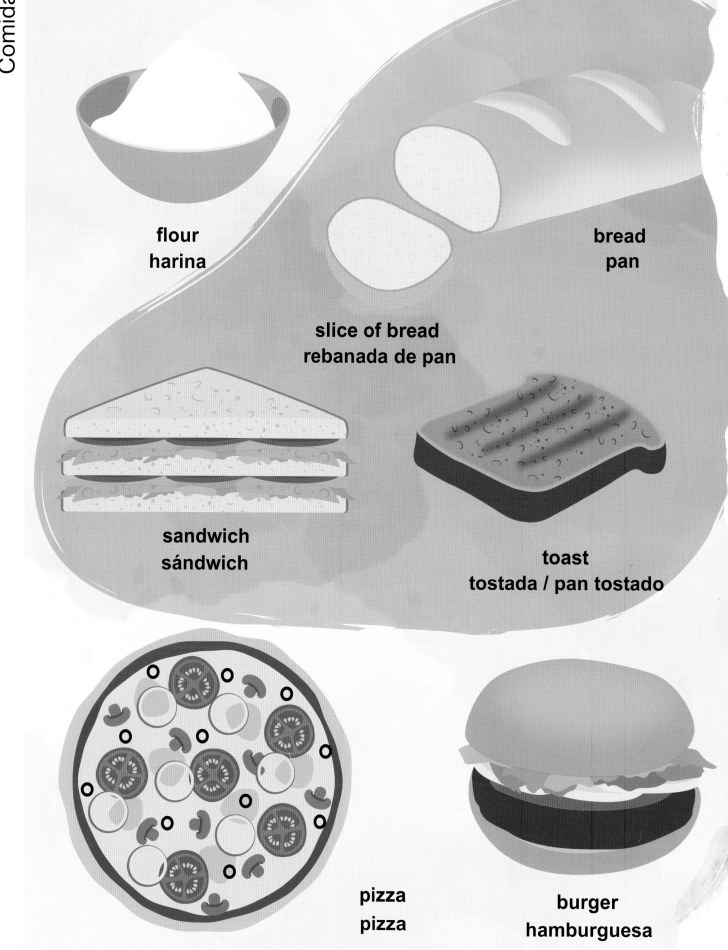

flour
harina

bread
pan

slice of bread
rebanada de pan

sandwich
sándwich

toast
tostada / pan tostado

pizza
pizza

burger
hamburguesa

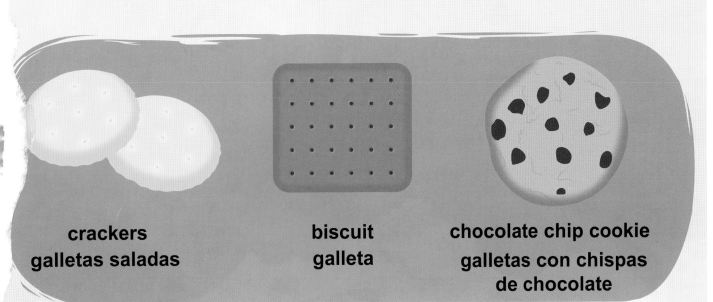

crackers
galletas saladas

biscuit
galleta

chocolate chip cookie
galletas con chispas
de chocolate

cake
tarta / pastel

pie
pay / pastel

pancakes
tortita / panqueques

almond
almendra

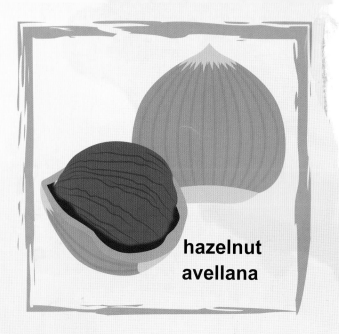

hazelnut
avellana

chestnut
castaña

pistachio
pistacho / pistache

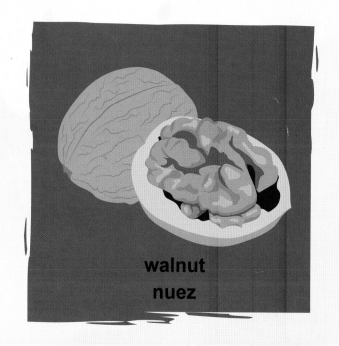

walnut
nuez

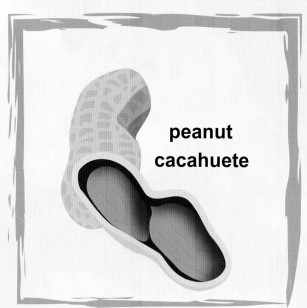

peanut
cacahuete

ground beef
carne molida

sausage
salchicha

fish
pescado

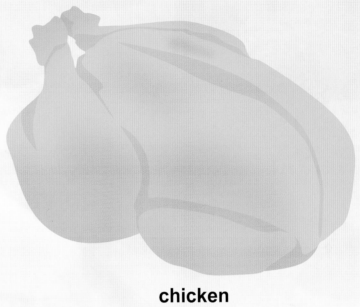

chicken
pollo

steak
bistec

egg
huevo

yolk
yema de huevo

egg white
clara de huevo

pasta
pasta

lentils
lenteja

rice
arroz

beans
judías / frijoles

66

honey
miel

canned food
comida enlatada

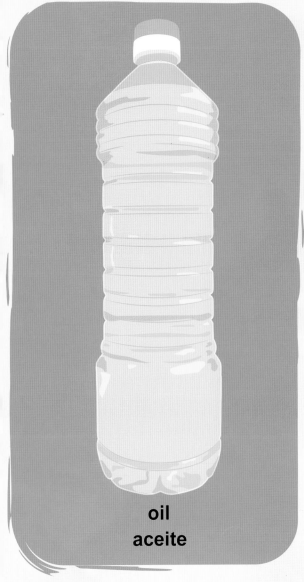

oil
aceite

olive
aceituna

olive oil
aceite de oliva

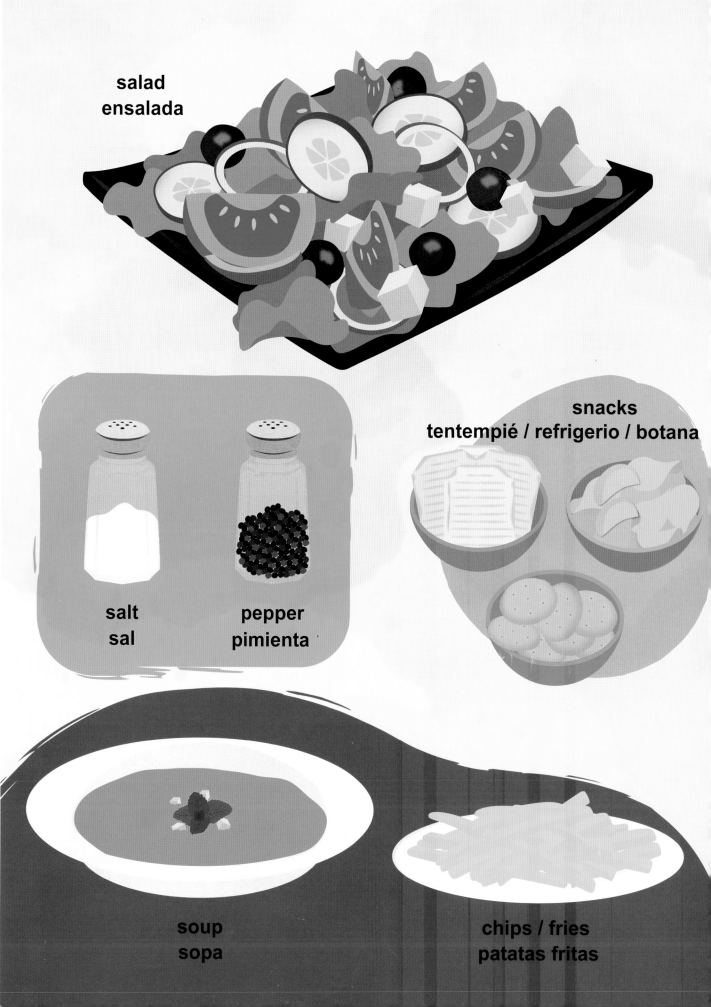

salad
ensalada

salt
sal

pepper
pimienta

snacks
tentempié / refrigerio / botana

soup
sopa

chips / fries
patatas fritas

sugar
azúcar

breakfast
desayuno

chocolate
chocolate

candy
golosinas

ice cream
helado

dessert
postre

popcorn
palomitas

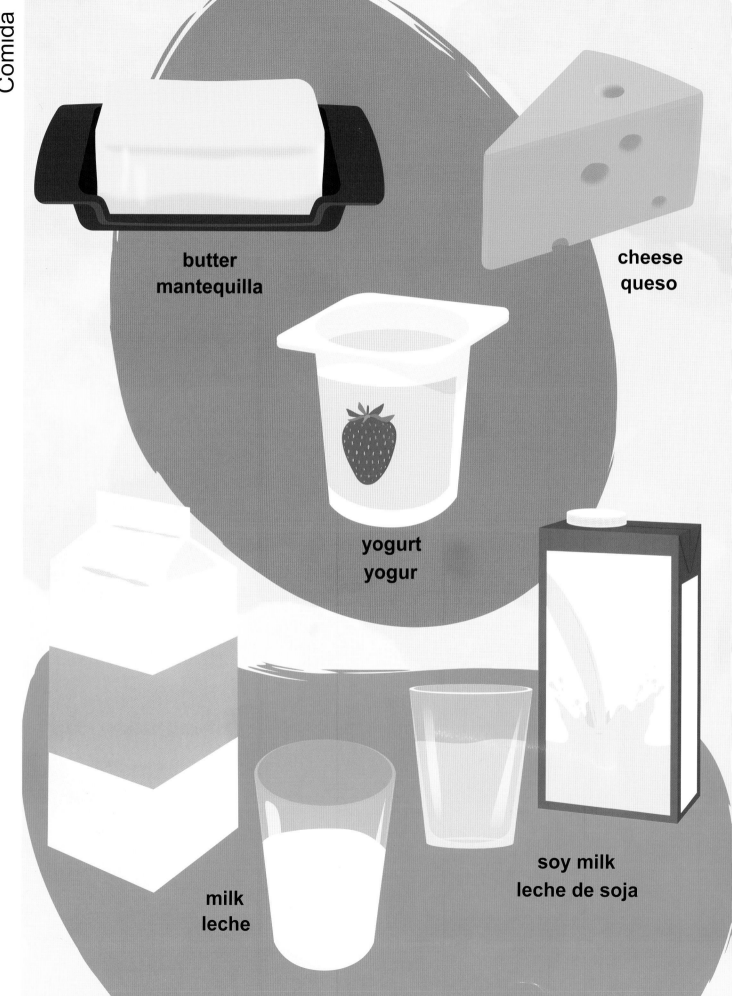

butter
mantequilla

cheese
queso

yogurt
yogur

milk
leche

soy milk
leche de soja

water
agua

fruit juice
jugo de fruta

lemonade
limonada

ice cube
cubo de hielo

orange juice
jugo de naranja

coffee
café

tea
té

car
coche

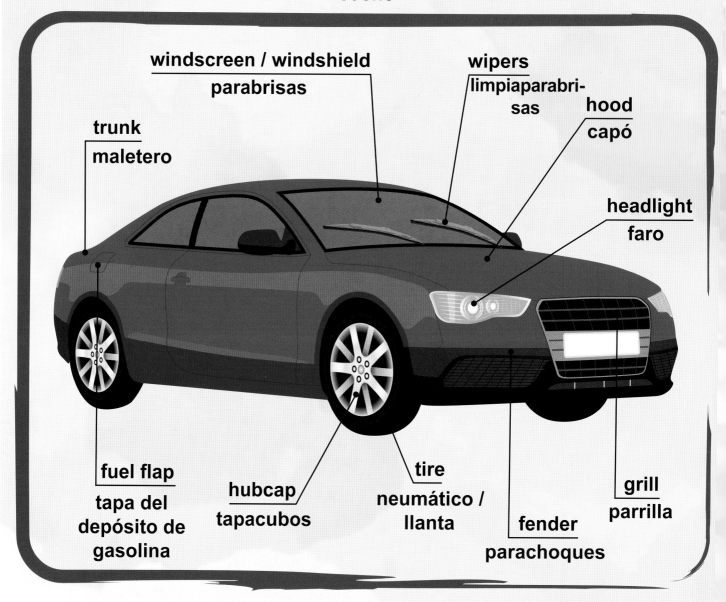

windscreen / windshield
parabrisas

wipers
limpiaparabri-
sas

hood
capó

trunk
maletero

headlight
faro

fuel flap
tapa del
depósito de
gasolina

hubcap
tapacubos

tire
neumático /
llanta

fender
parachoques

grill
parrilla

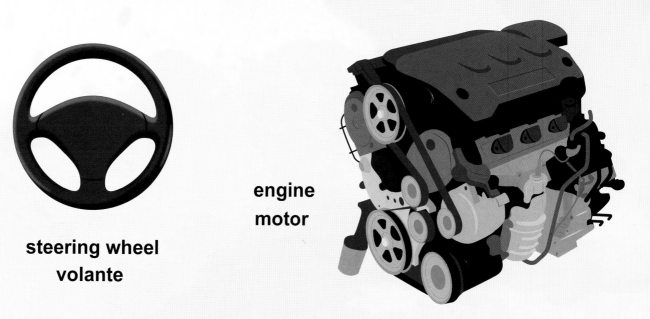

steering wheel
volante

engine
motor

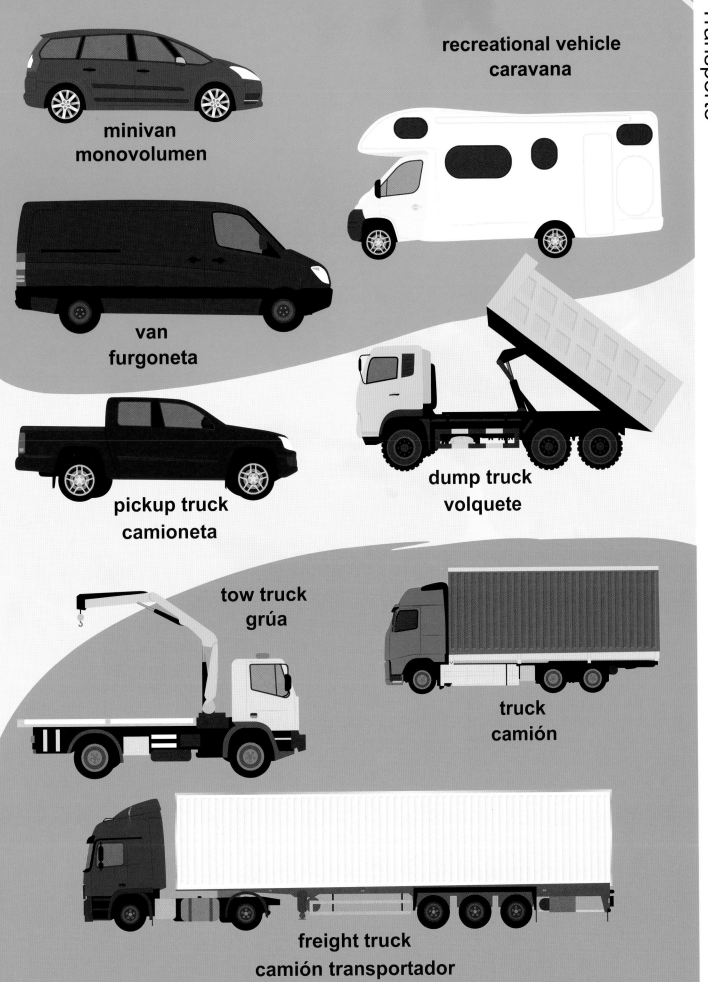

minivan
monovolumen

recreational vehicle
caravana

van
furgoneta

dump truck
volquete

pickup truck
camioneta

tow truck
grúa

truck
camión

freight truck
camión transportador

bulldozer
topadora

digger
excavadora

forklift
carretilla elevadora

tractor
tractor

police car
coche patrulla

fire truck
camión de bomberos

race car
coche de carreras

ambulance
ambulancia

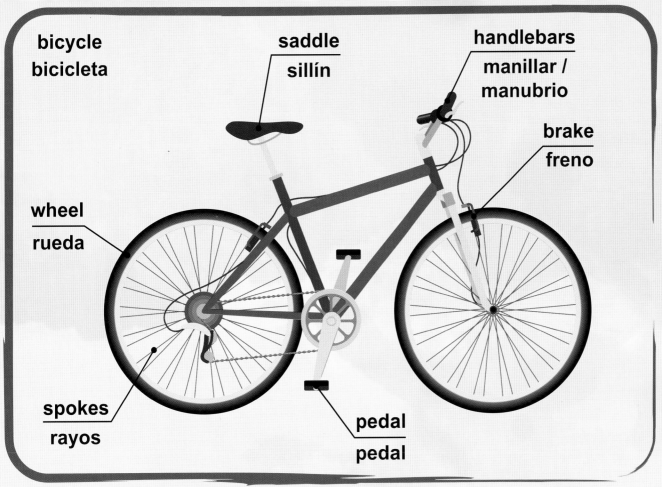

bicycle
bicicleta

saddle
sillín

handlebars
manillar /
manubrio

brake
freno

wheel
rueda

spokes
rayos

pedal
pedal

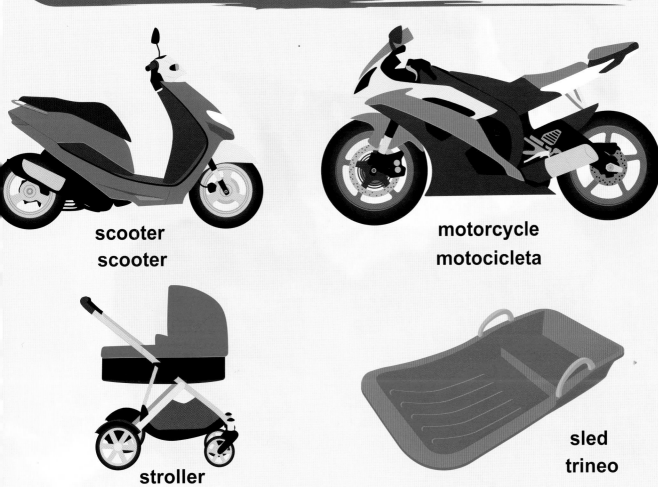

scooter
scooter

motorcycle
motocicleta

stroller
carriola

sled
trineo

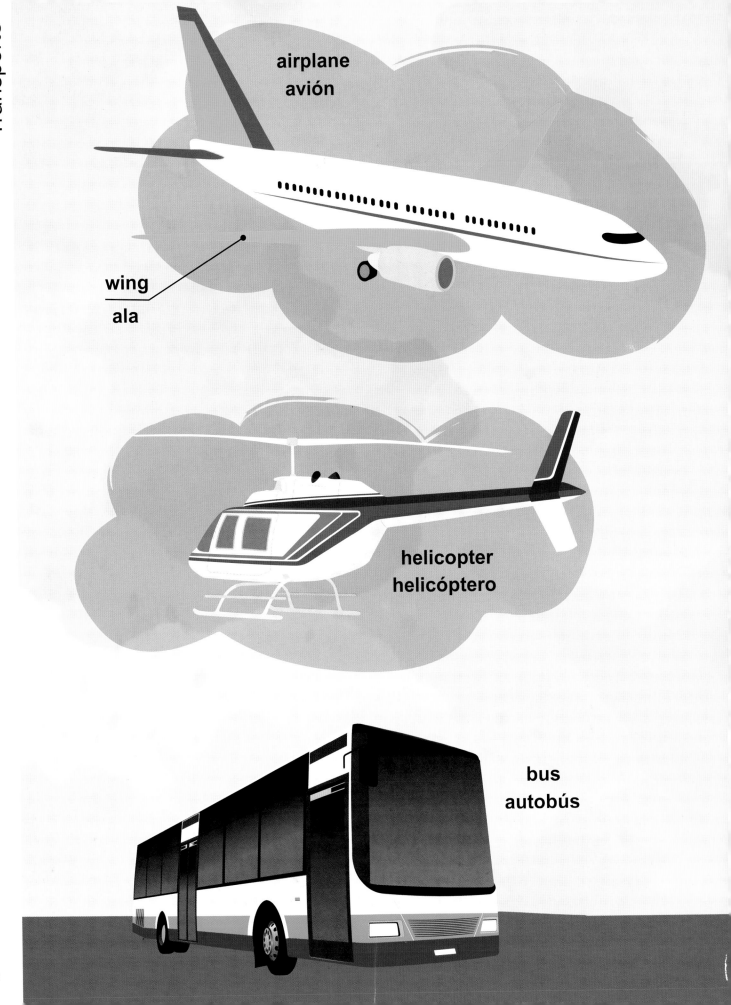

airplane
avión

wing
ala

helicopter
helicóptero

bus
autobús

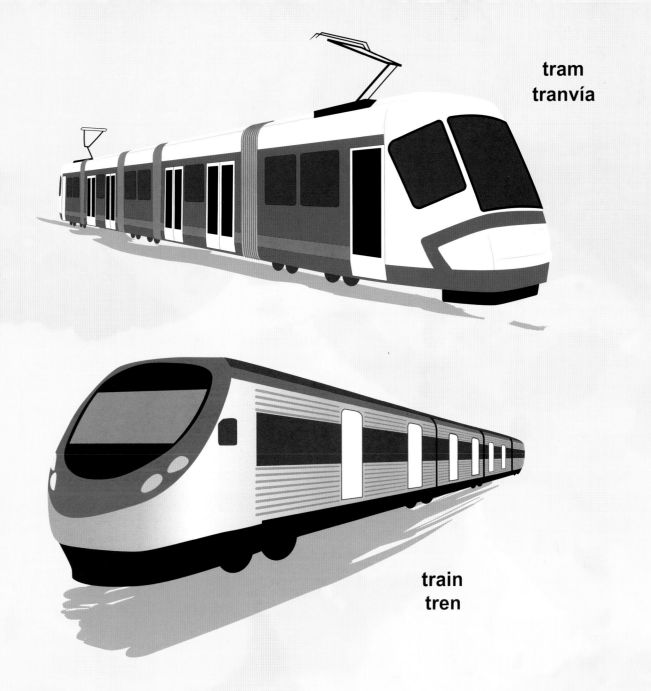

tram
tranvía

train
tren

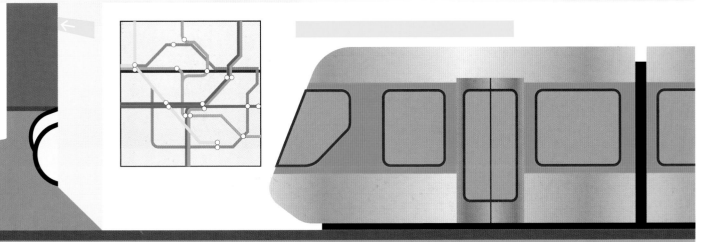

underground / subway
metro

container ship
carguero

cruise ship
crucero

yacht
yate

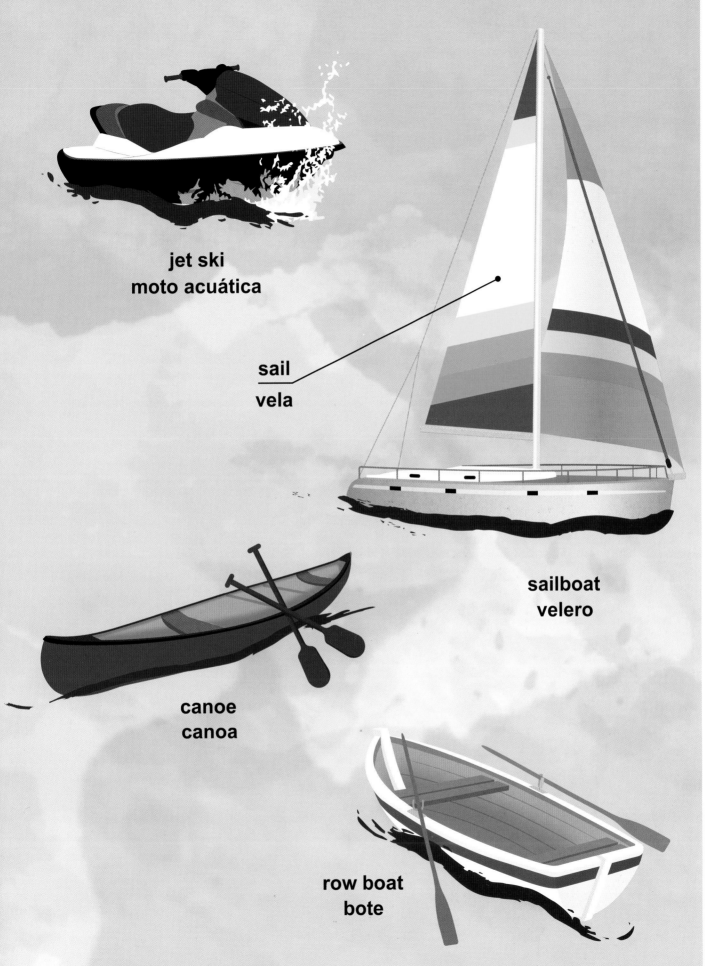

jet ski
moto acuática

sail
vela

sailboat
velero

canoe
canoa

row boat
bote

airport
aeropuerto

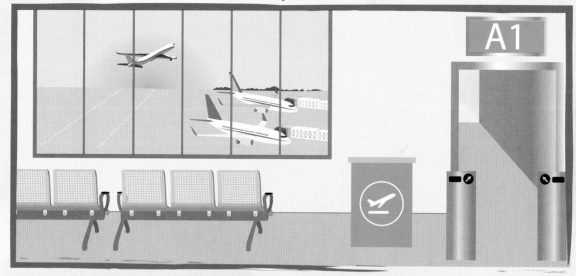

street
calle

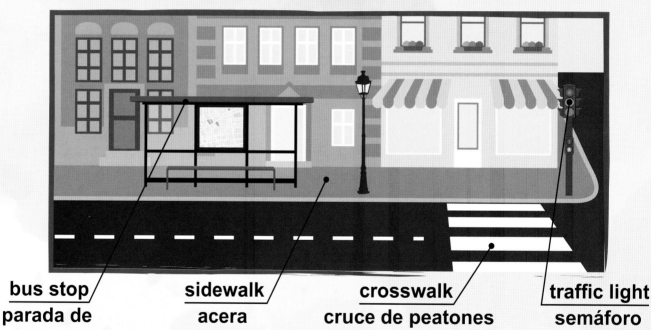

bus stop
parada de
autobús

sidewalk
acera

crosswalk
cruce de peatones

traffic light
semáforo

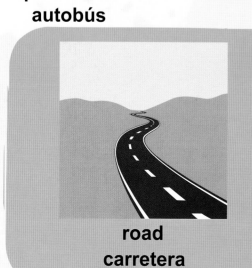

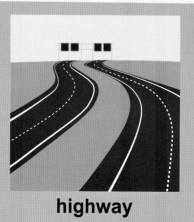

road
carretera

highway
autopista

traffic
tráfico

garage
garaje

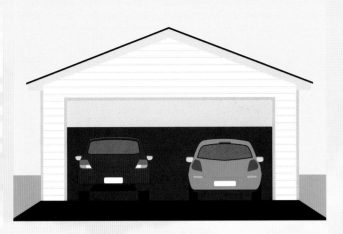

petrol station / gas station
gasolinera

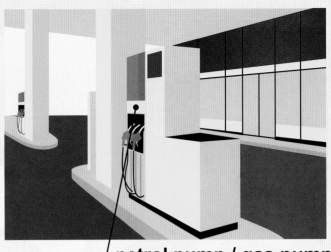

petrol pump / gas pump
bomba de gasolina

train station
estación ferroviaria

railroad track
vía de tren

bridge
puente

pier
embarcadero

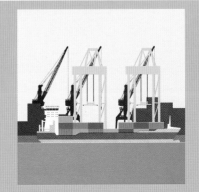

port
puerto

fuchsia
fucsia

camellia
camelia

daisy
margarita

cotton
algodón

bud
capullo

begonia
begonia

carnation
clavel

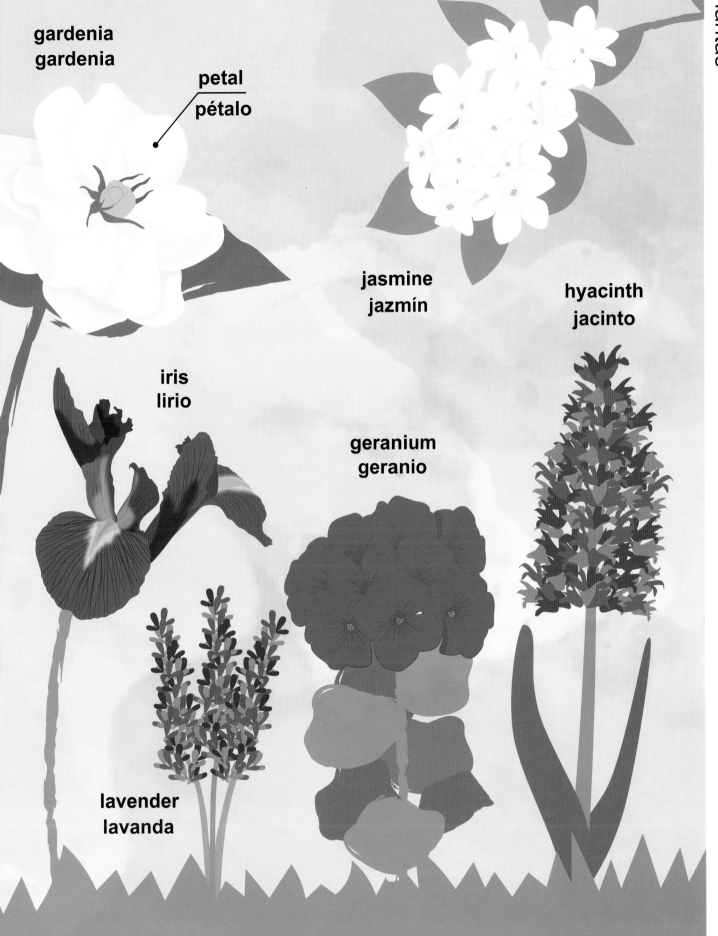

gardenia
gardenia

petal
pétalo

jasmine
jazmín

hyacinth
jacinto

iris
lirio

geranium
geranio

lavender
lavanda

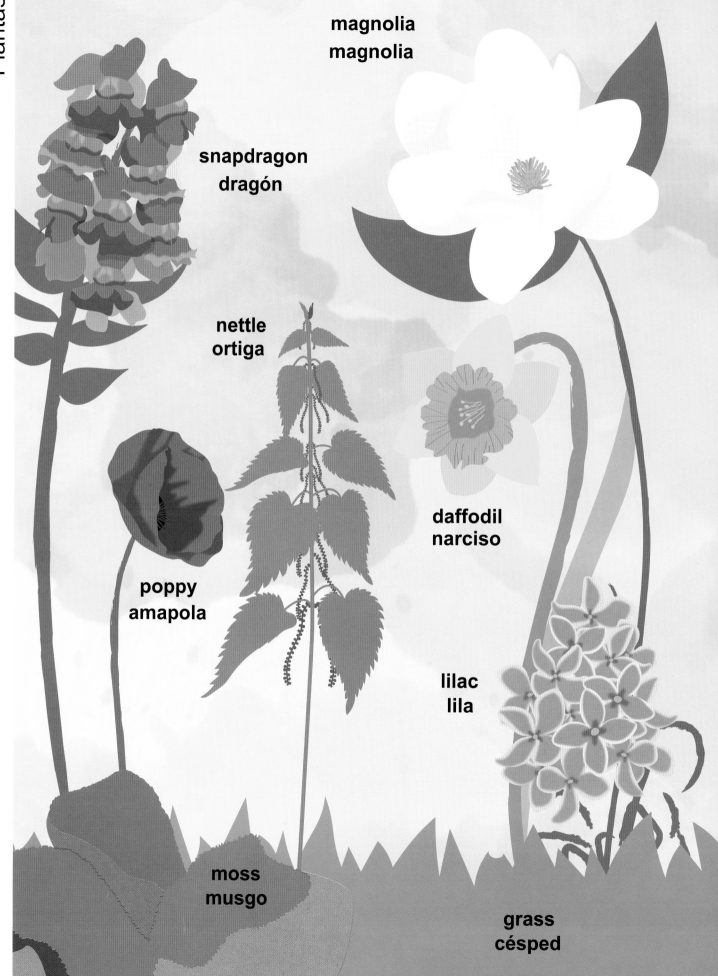

magnolia
magnolia

snapdragon
dragón

nettle
ortiga

poppy
amapola

daffodil
narciso

lilac
lila

moss
musgo

grass
césped

orchid
orquídea

rose
rosa

sunflower
girasol

tulip
tulipán

snowdrop
campanilla
de invierno

water lily
nenúfar /
lirio de agua

pine cone
piñón

oats
avena

wheat
trigo

rye
centeno

palm tree
palmera

cactus
cactus

grape tree
viña

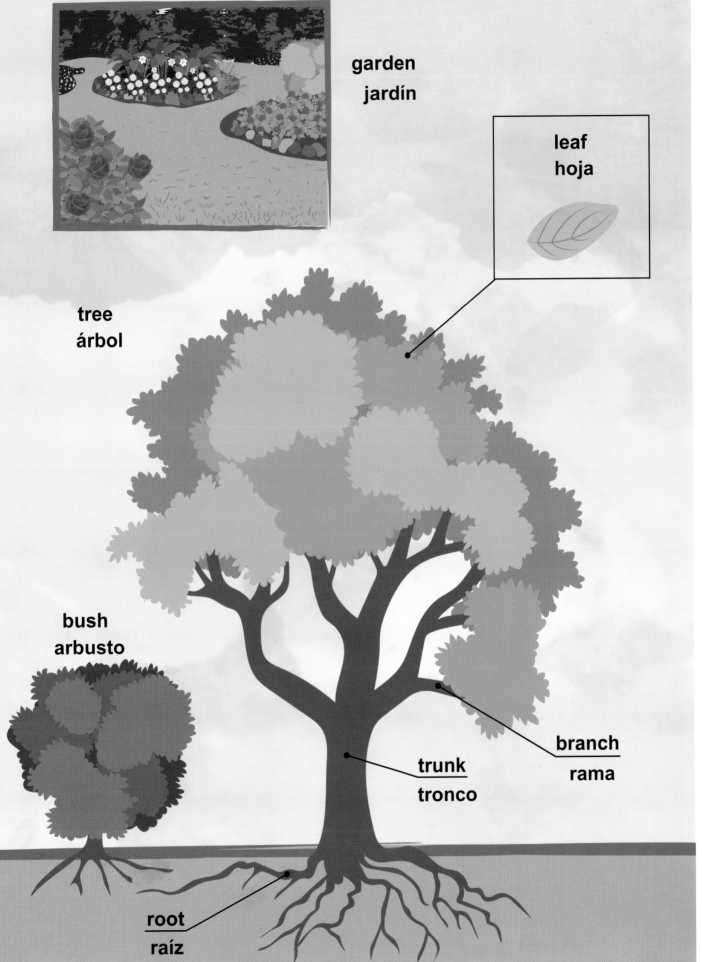

garden
jardín

leaf
hoja

tree
árbol

bush
arbusto

branch
rama

trunk
tronco

root
raíz

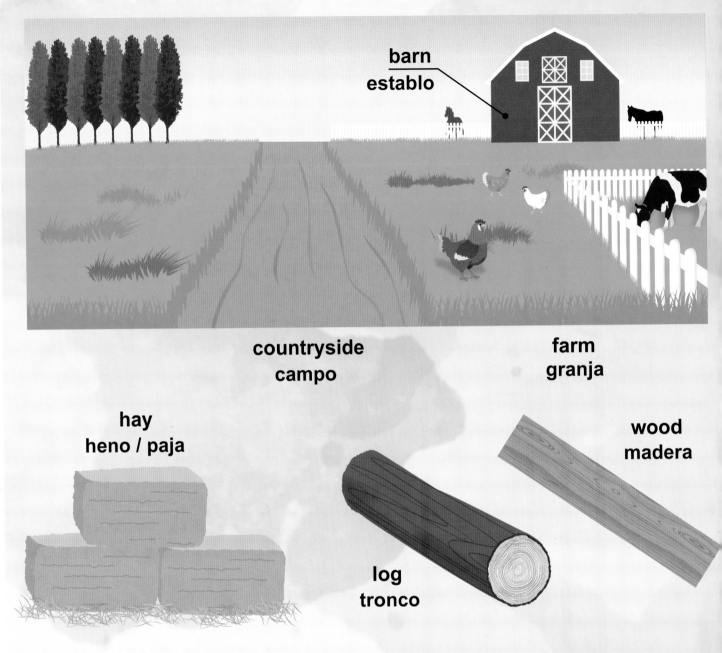

barn
establo

countryside
campo

farm
granja

hay
heno / paja

wood
madera

log
tronco

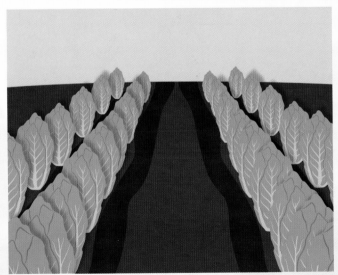

harvest
cosecha

field
campo

island
isla

sand
arena

beach
playa

lake
lago

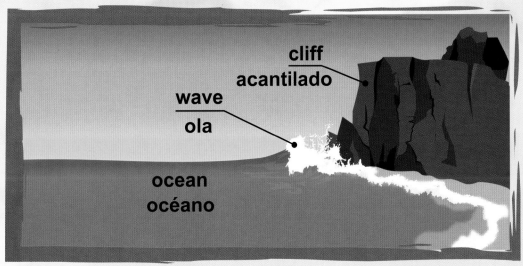

cliff
acantilado

wave
ola

ocean
océano

coast
costa

wetland
pantano

dam
dique / presa

waterfall
cascada

forest
bosque

path
camino

desert
desierto

cave
cueva

jungle
selva

soil
tierra

fossil
fósil

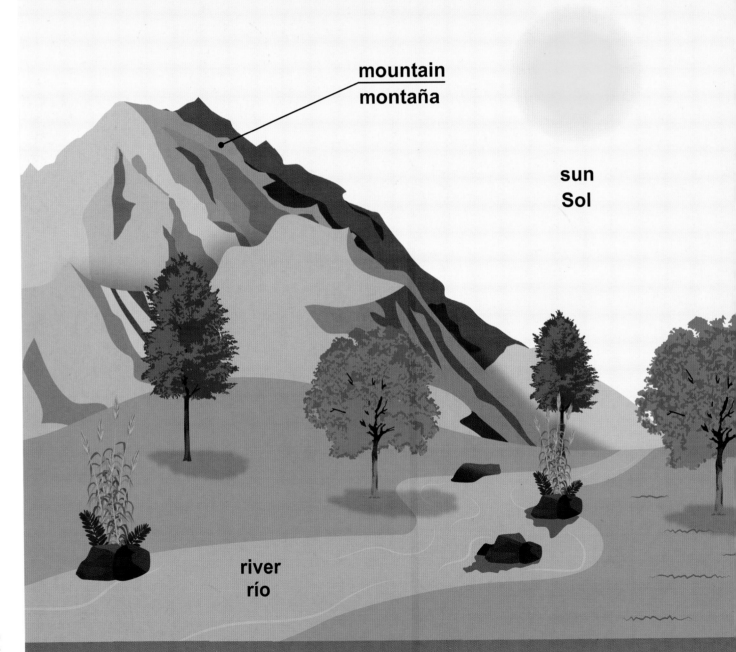

mountain
montaña

sun
Sol

river
río

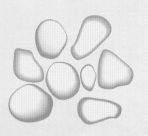

pebbles
guijarro /
piedrecillas

stone
piedra

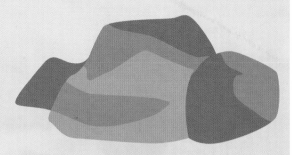

rock
roca

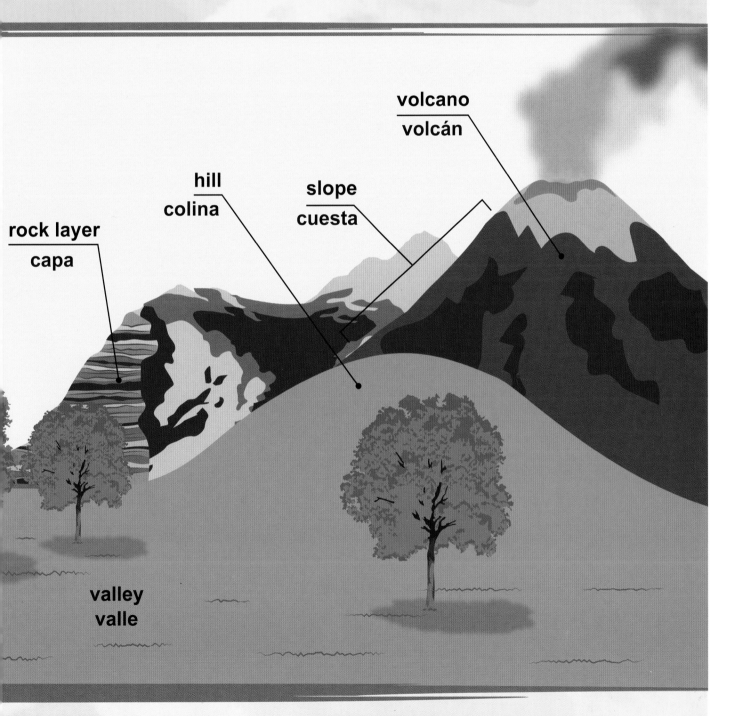

volcano
volcán

hill
colina

slope
cuesta

rock layer
capa

valley
valle

disaster
desastre

hurricane
huracán

flood
inundación

earthquake
terremoto

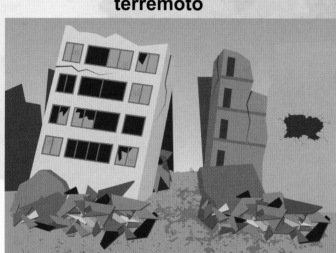

tornado
tornado

fire
fuego

flame
llama

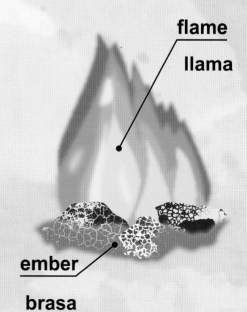

ember
brasa

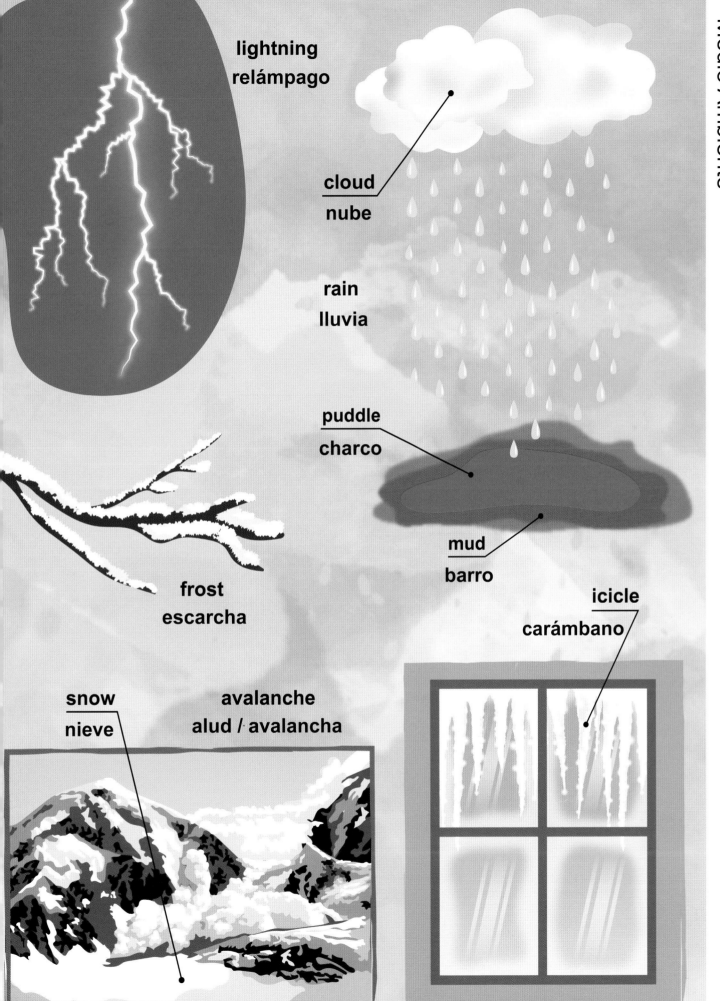

lightning
relámpago

cloud
nube

rain
lluvia

puddle
charco

mud
barro

frost
escarcha

icicle
carámbano

snow
nieve

avalanche
alud / avalancha

continents
continentes

North America
Norteamérica

Europe
Europa

South America
Sudamérica

Antarctica
Antártica

Asia
Asia

Africa
África

Australia
Australia

solar system
sistema solar

Moon
Luna

Venus
Venus

Mercury
Mercurio

Earth
Tierra

Neptune
Neptuno

Mars
Marte

Sun
Sol

Uranus
Urano

Saturn
Saturno

Jupiter
Júpiter

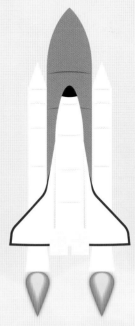

galaxy
galaxia

space shuttle
transbordador
espacial

space station
estación espacial

satellite dish
antena parabólica

astronaut
astronauta

American football
fútbol americano

basketball
baloncesto

weightlifting
levantamiento de pesas

archery
tiro con arco

judo
judo

wrestling
lucha

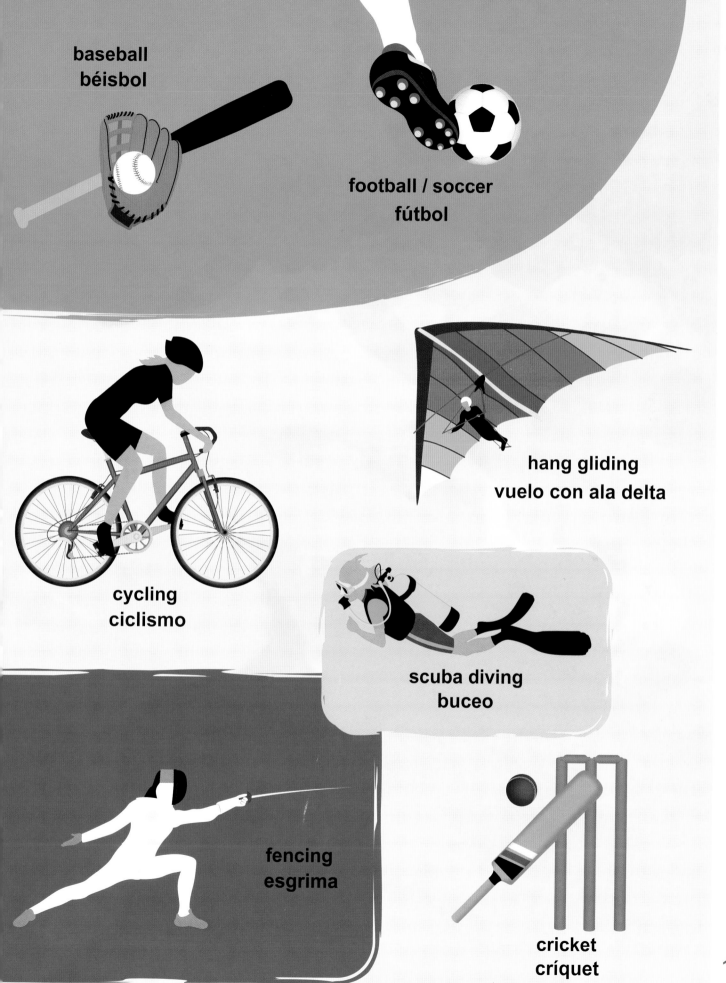

baseball
béisbol

football / soccer
fútbol

cycling
ciclismo

hang gliding
vuelo con ala delta

scuba diving
buceo

fencing
esgrima

cricket
críquet

marathon
maratón

stadium
estadio

sprint
carrera de
velocidad

high jump
salto de altura

javelin throw
lanzamiento
de jabalina

hurdles
carrera de vallas

waterpolo
waterpolo

swimming pool
piscina

swimming
natación

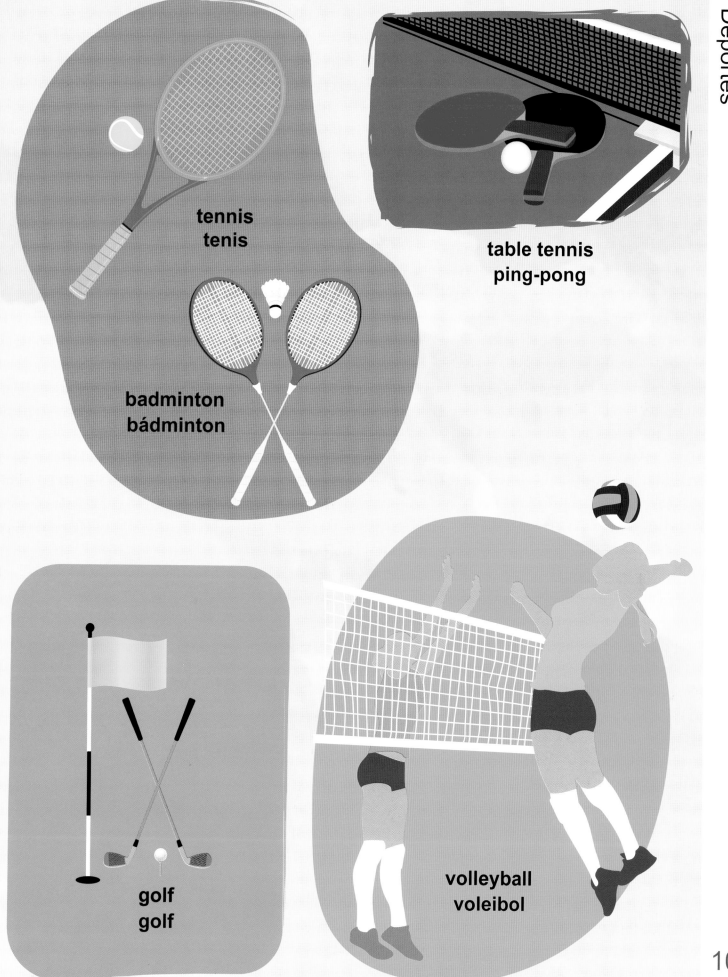

tennis
tenis

table tennis
ping-pong

badminton
bádminton

golf
golf

volleyball
voleibol

103

mountain climbing
alpinismo

snowboarding
surf de nieve

ice hockey
hockey sobre hielo

skiing
esquí

rowing
remo

sailing
vela

rafting
descenso de ríos

hiking
senderismo

horse riding
equitación

sleeping bag
saco de dormir

compass
brújula

tent
tienda de
campaña

canvas
lienzo

painting
cuadro

palette
paleta

frame
marco

bust
busto

easel
caballete

ballet
ballet

sculpture
escultura

auditorium
auditorio

orchestra
orquestra

stage
escenario

concert
concierto

audience
público

cinema
cine

museum
museo

theater
teatro

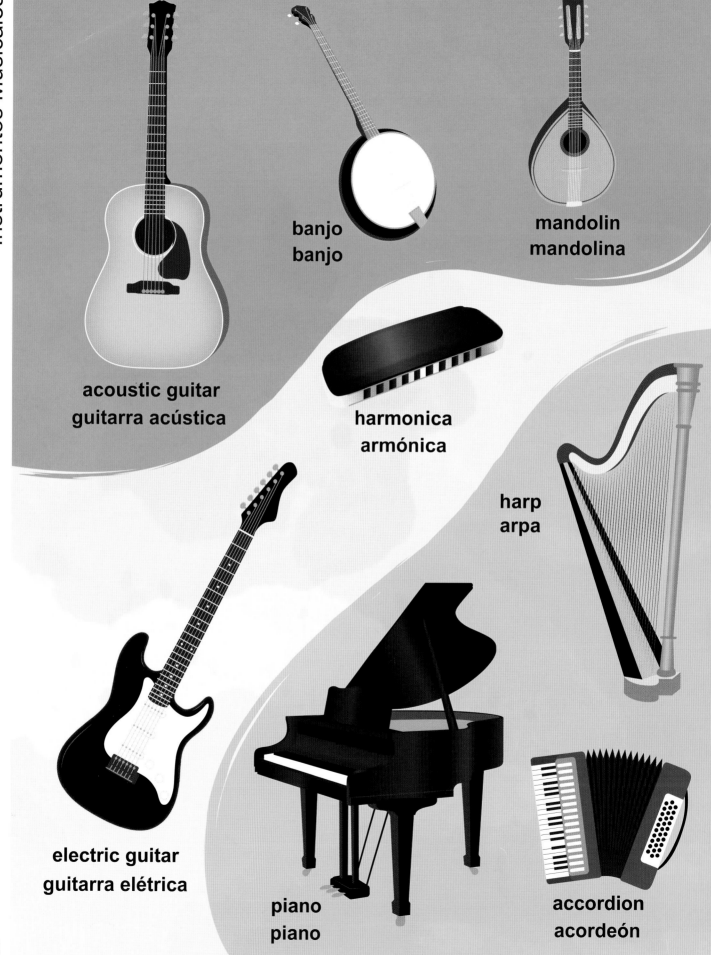

banjo
banjo

mandolin
mandolina

acoustic guitar
guitarra acústica

harmonica
armónica

harp
arpa

electric guitar
guitarra elétrica

piano
piano

accordion
acordeón

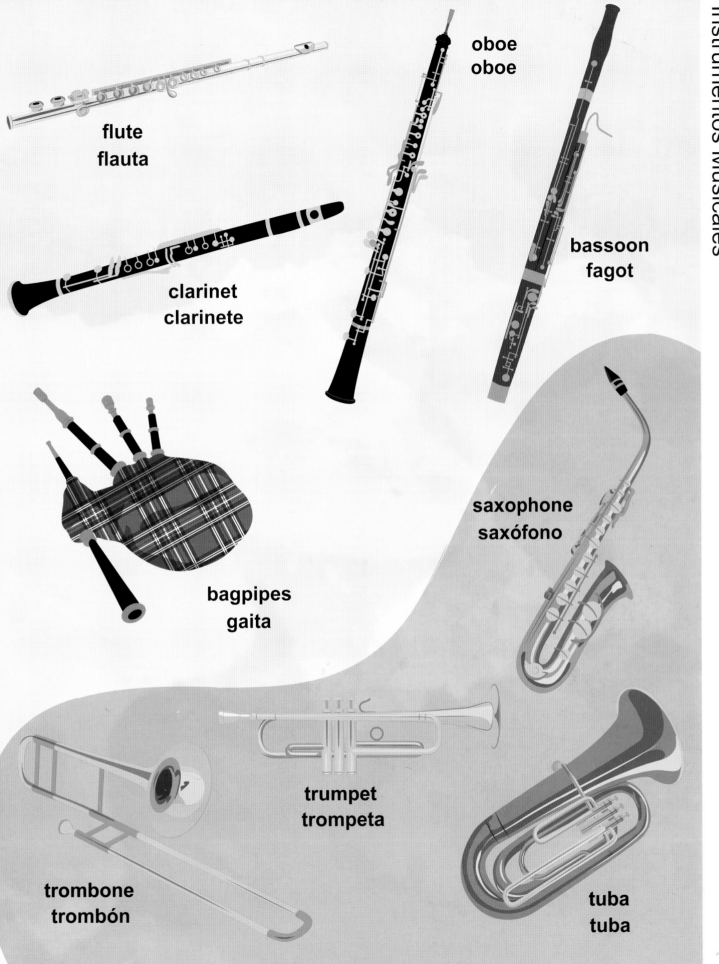

flute
flauta

oboe
oboe

bassoon
fagot

clarinet
clarinete

bagpipes
gaita

saxophone
saxófono

trumpet
trompeta

trombone
trombón

tuba
tuba

drum kit
batería

snare drum
caja clara /
tarola

cymbal
platillo

bass drum
bombo

drumsticks
baquetas

tambourine
pandereta

bongo drums
bongós

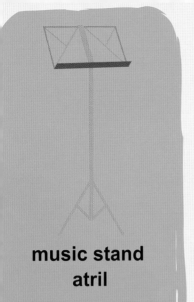

music stand
atril

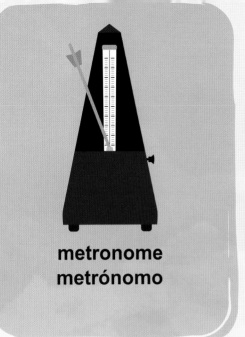

metronome
metrónomo

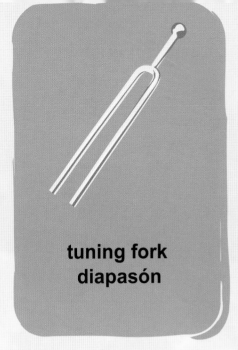

tuning fork
diapasón

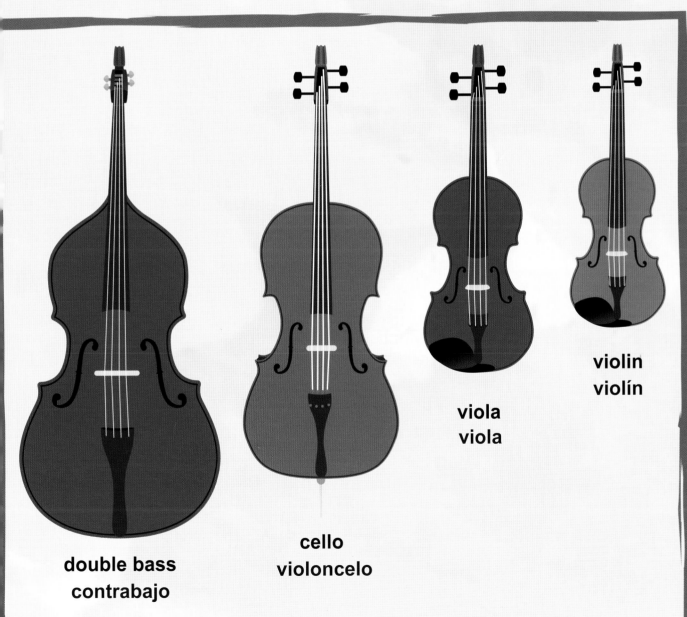

double bass
contrabajo

cello
violoncelo

viola
viola

violin
violín

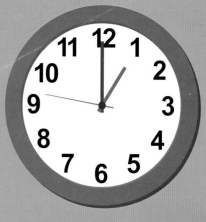

one o'clock
una en punto

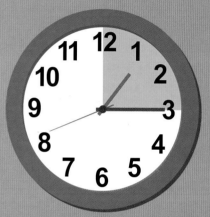

one fifteen /
quarter past one
la una y cuarto

hour hand
manecilla
de la hora

minute hand
minutero

second hand
segundero

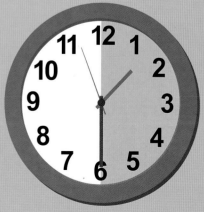

one thirty /
half past one
la una y media

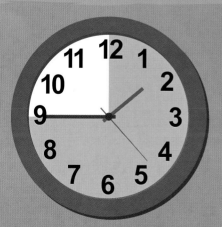

one forty-five /
quarter to two
las dos menos cuarto

dawn
alba

sunrise
amanecer

evening
tarde

dusk
anochecer

night
noche

midnight
medianoche

Time
Hora

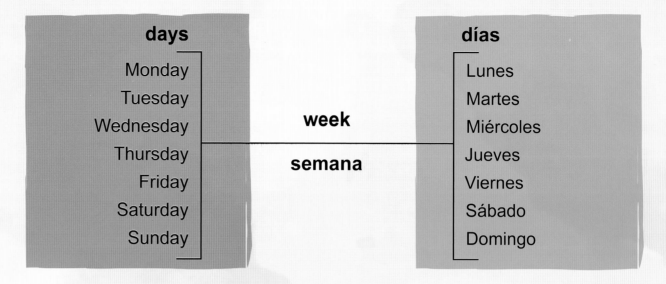

days	week / semana	días
Monday		Lunes
Tuesday		Martes
Wednesday		Miércoles
Thursday		Jueves
Friday		Viernes
Saturday		Sábado
Sunday		Domingo

months	year / año	meses
January		Enero
February		Febrero
March		Marzo
April		Abril
May		Mayo
June		Junio
July		Julio
August		Agosto
September		Septiembre
October		Octubre
November		Noviembre
December		Diciembre

**2016
2026**
decade
década

**2016
2116**
century
siglo

**2016
3016**
millennium
milenio

seasons
estaciones

spring
primavera

summer
verano

fall
otoño

winter
invierno

classroom
aula

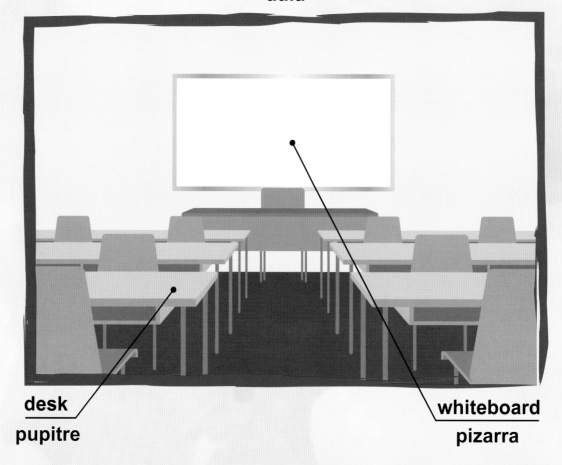

desk
pupitre

whiteboard
pizarra

library
biblioteca

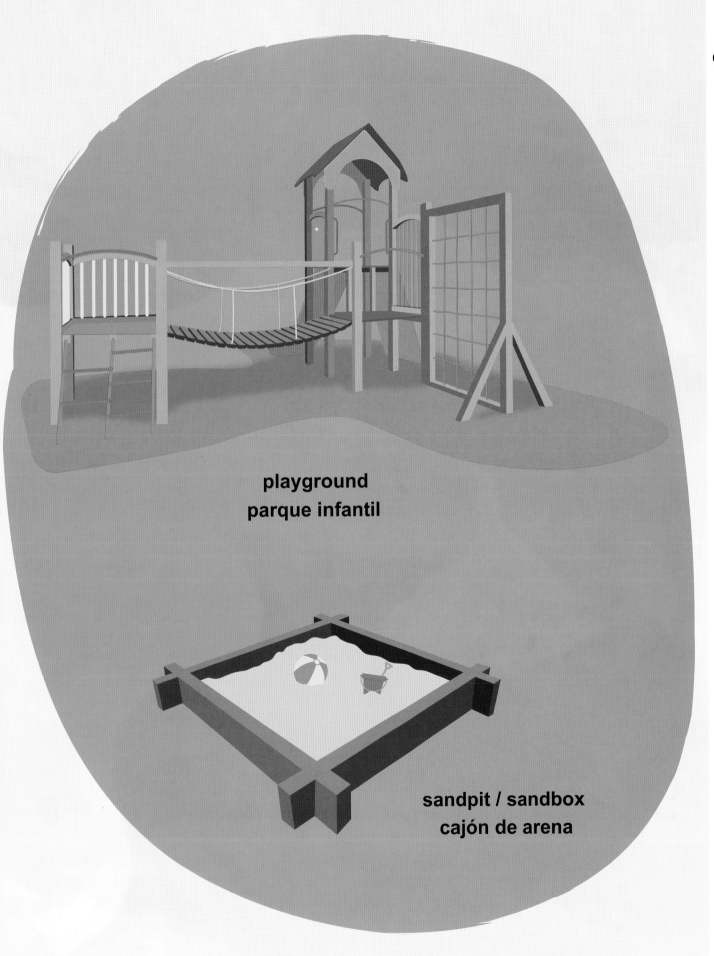

playground
parque infantil

sandpit / sandbox
cajón de arena

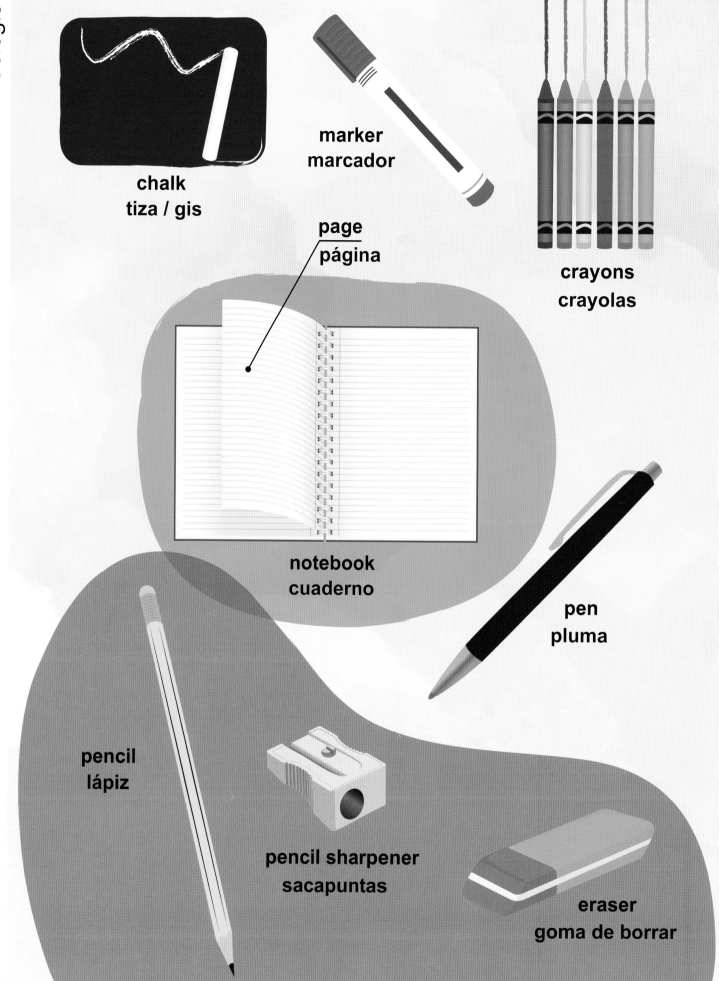

chalk
tiza / gis

marker
marcador

crayons
crayolas

page
página

notebook
cuaderno

pen
pluma

pencil
lápiz

pencil sharpener
sacapuntas

eraser
goma de borrar

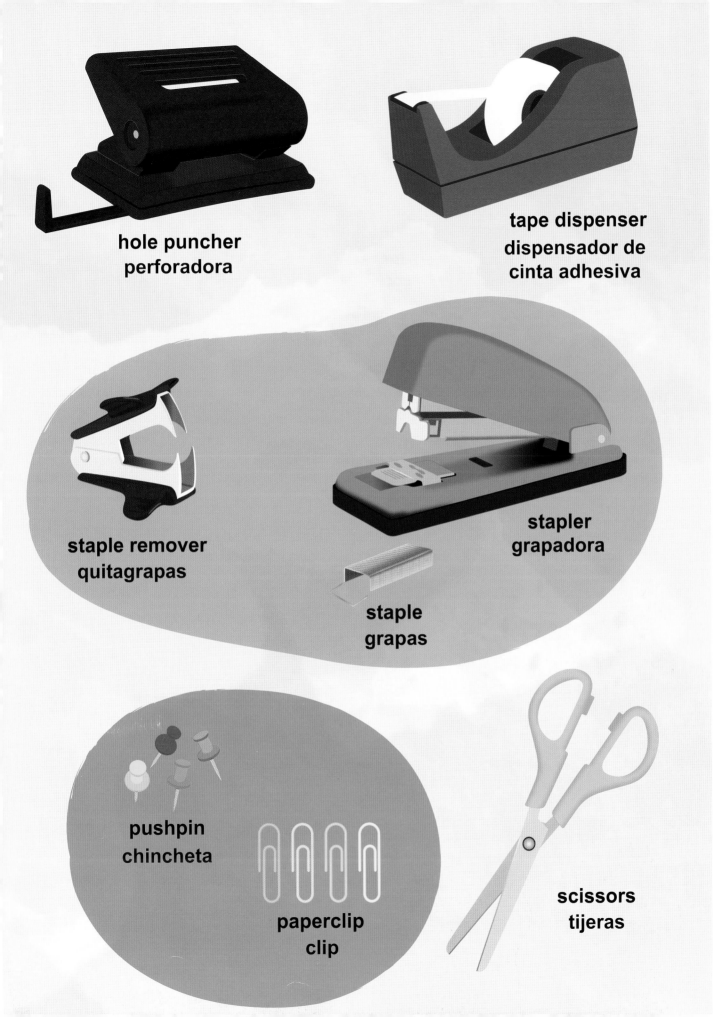

hole puncher
perforadora

tape dispenser
dispensador de
cinta adhesiva

staple remover
quitagrapas

stapler
grapadora

staple
grapas

pushpin
chincheta

paperclip
clip

scissors
tijeras

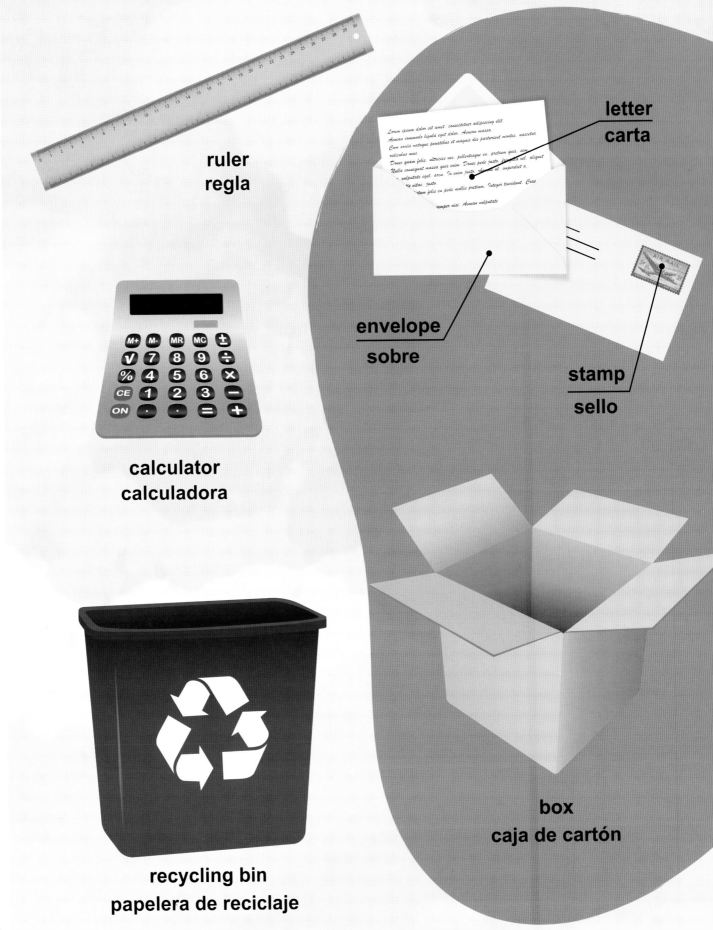

ruler
regla

letter
carta

envelope
sobre

stamp
sello

calculator
calculadora

box
caja de cartón

recycling bin
papelera de reciclaje

globe
globo terráqueo

telescope
telescopio

microscope
microscopio

magnifying glass
lupa

magnet
imán

0
zero
cero

1

1st
first
primero

one
uno

2

2nd
second
segundo

two
dos

3

3rd
third
tercero

three
tres

4

4th
fourth
cuarto

four
cuatro

5 **5**th
fifth
quinto
five
cinco

6 **6**th
sixth
sexto
six
seis

7 **7**th
seventh
séptimo
seven
siete

8 **8**th
eighth
octavo
eight
ocho

9 **9**th
ninth
noveno
nine
nueve

10
ten
diez

10th — tenth
décimo

11
eleven
once

11th — eleventh
undécimo

12
twelve
doce

12th — twelfth
duodécimo

13
thirteen
trece

13th — thirteenth
decimotercero

14
fourteen
catorce

14th — fourteenth
decimocuatro

15

15th

fifteen
quince

fifteenth
decimoquinto

16

16th

sixteen
dieciséis

sixteenth
decimosexto

17

17th

seventeen
diecisiete

seventeenth
decimoséptimo

18

18th

eighteen
dieciocho

eighteenth
decimoctavo

19

19th

nineteen
diecinueve

nineteenth
decimonoveno

20 twenty
veinte

20th twentieth
vigésimo

30 thirty
treinta

30th thirtieth
trigésimo/a

40 forty
cuarenta

40th fortieth
cuadragésimo/a

50 fifty
cincuenta

50th fiftieth
quincuagésimo/a

60 sixty
sesenta

60th sixtieth
sexagésimo/a

70 seventy
setenta

70th seventieth
septuagésimo/a

80 eighty
ochenta

80th eightieth
octogésimo/a

90 ninety
noventa

90th ninetieth
nonagésimo/a

100 one hundred
cien

100th one hundredth
número cien

200 two hundred
doscientos

500 five hundred
quinientos

800 eight hundred
ochocientos

1,000 one thousand
mil

100,000 one hundred thousand
cien mil

1,000,000 one million
un millón

127

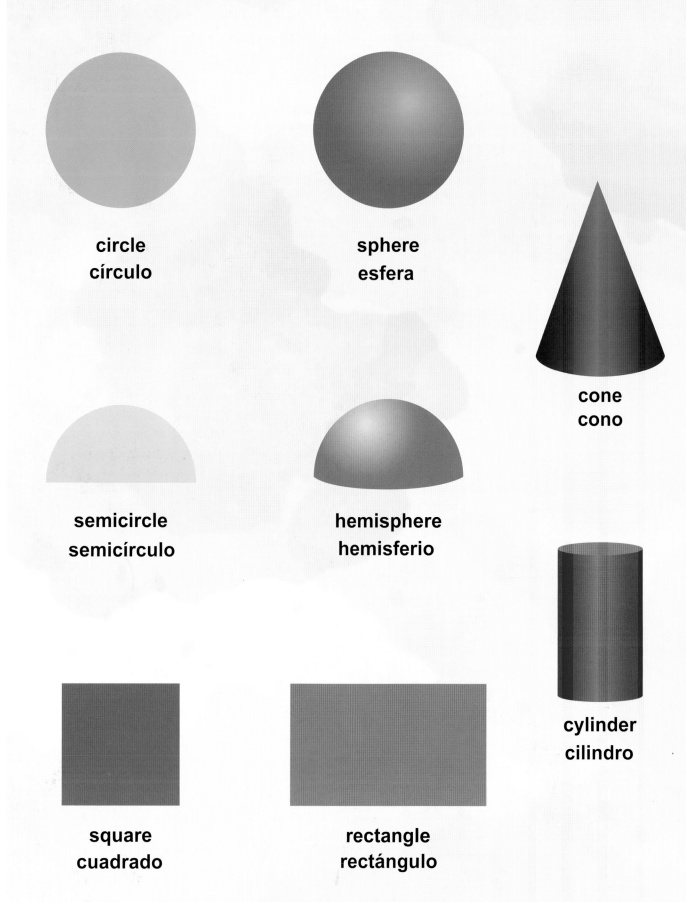

circle
círculo

sphere
esfera

cone
cono

semicircle
semicírculo

hemisphere
hemisferio

cylinder
cilindro

square
cuadrado

rectangle
rectángulo

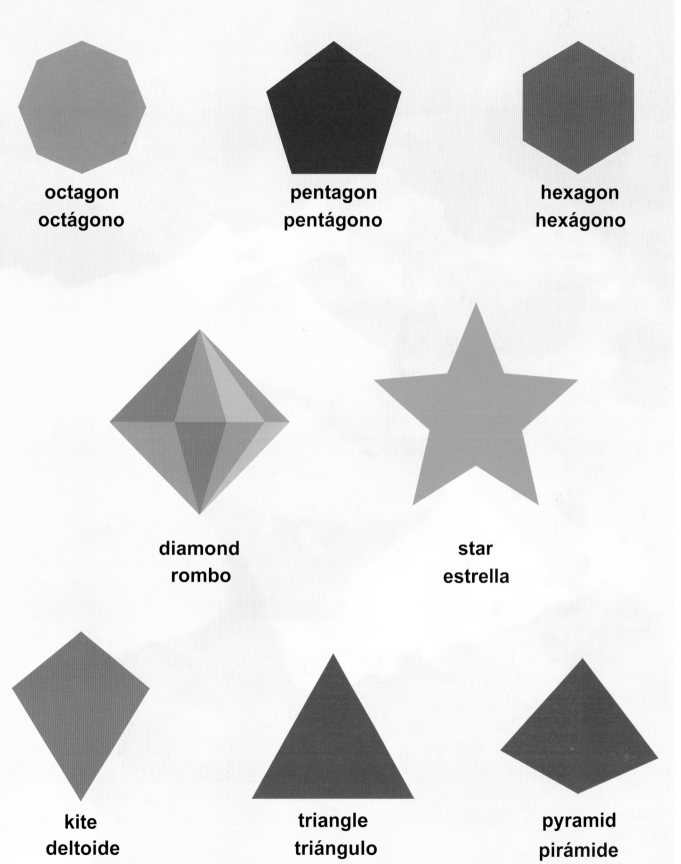

octagon
octágono

pentagon
pentágono

hexagon
hexágono

diamond
rombo

star
estrella

kite
deltoide

triangle
triángulo

pyramid
pirámide

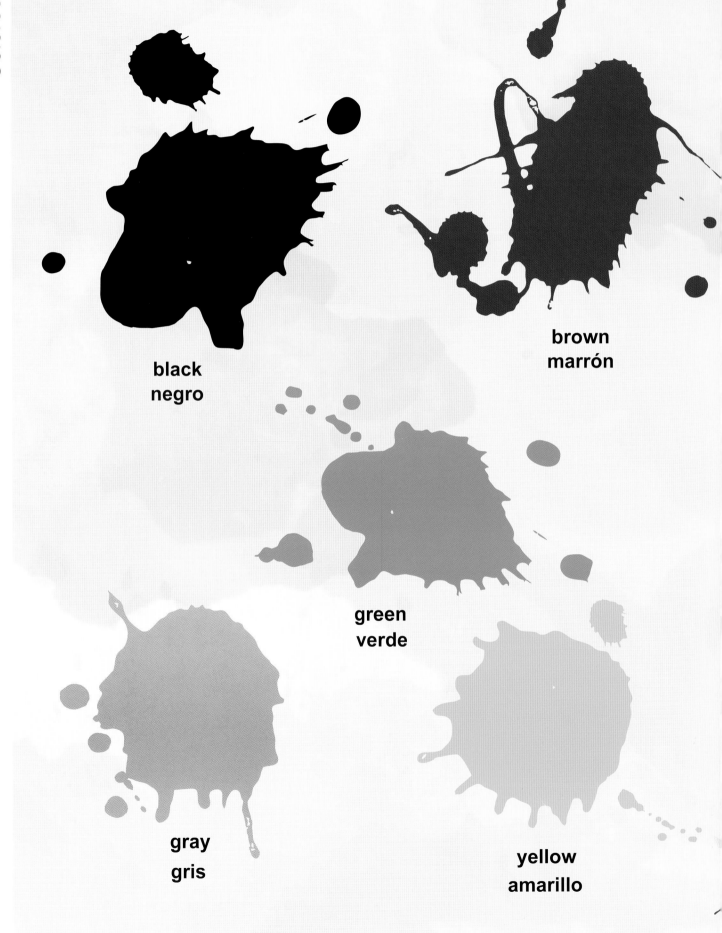

**black
negro**

**brown
marrón**

**green
verde**

**gray
gris**

**yellow
amarillo**

130

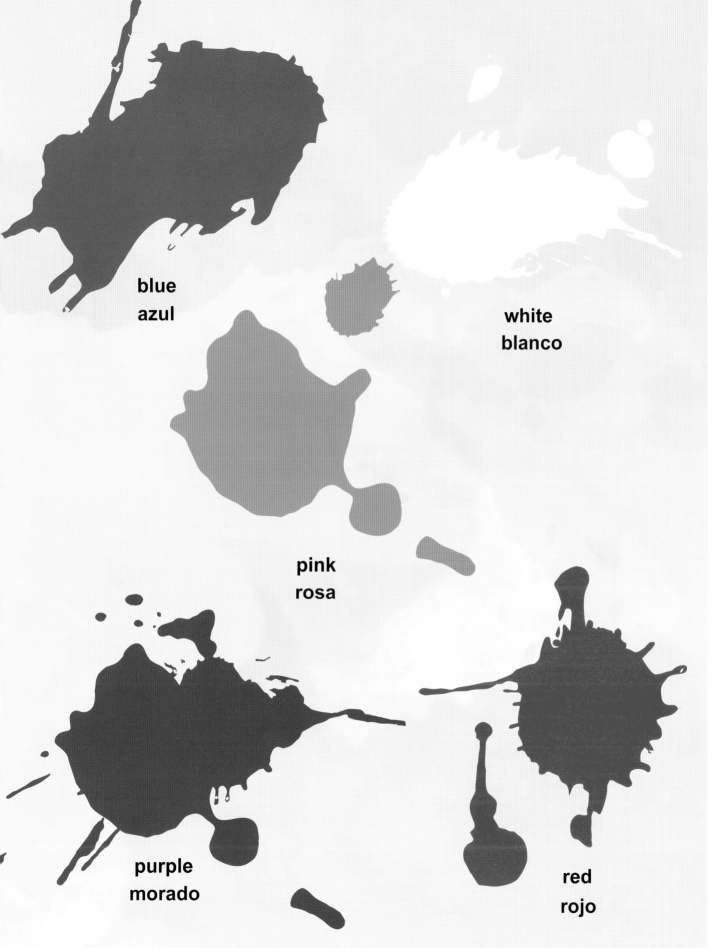

blue
azul

white
blanco

pink
rosa

purple
morado

red
rojo

It's
apostrophe
apóstrofo

Yes,
comma
coma

like:
colon
dos puntos

self-confidence
hyphen
guión

after...
ellipsis
puntos suspensivos

won!
exclamation point
signo de admiración

When?
question mark
signo de interrogación

end.
period
punto

"One day,"
quotation marks
comillas

(almost)
parentheses
paréntesis

open;
semicolon
punto y coma

'good'
single quotation marks
comillas

$3+1$

plus sign
signo de más

$7-3$

minus sign
signo de menos

$8\div2$

division sign
signo de división

2×2

multiplication sign
signo de multiplicar

$\sqrt{16}$

square root sign
signo de raíz cuadrada

$=4$

equal sign
signo de igual

25%

percent sign
signo de porcentaje

earth & space

ampersand
y

he/she/they

forward slash
diagonal

html\n

backslash
diagonal invertida

info@milet.com

at sign
arroba